# Perfection!

## LSU Tigers National Champions

**JOSH CRUTCHMER,** *Cover Design*
**NICKY BRILLOWSKI,** *Book Design*

© 2020 KCI Sports Publishing
All rights reserved. Except for use in a review, the reproduction or
utilization of this work in any form or by any electronic, mechanical, or other means,
now known or hereafter invented, including xerography, photocopying, and recording,
and in any information storage and retrieval system, is forbidden without the
written permission of the publisher.

ISBN: 978-1-940056-79-1 (HC)
978-1-940056-74-6 (PB)

Printed in the United States of America

This is an unofficial publication. This book is in no way affiliated with,
licensed by or endorsed by Louisiana State University.

| | |
|---|---|
| **INTRO** | **4** |
| National Championship \| **CLEMSON** | **8** |
| Regular Season \| **GEORGIA SOUTHERN** | **20** |
| Regular Season \| **TEXAS** | **24** |
| Regular Season \| **NORTHWESTERN STATE** | **32** |
| LSU Feature \| **JOE BURROW** | **36** |
| Regular Season \| **VANDERBILT** | **42** |
| Regular Season \| **UTAH STATE** | **48** |
| Regular Season \| **FLORIDA** | **52** |
| LSU Feature \| **GRANT DELPIT** | **58** |
| Regular Season \| **MISSISSIPPI STATE** | **62** |
| Regular Season \| **AUBURN** | **68** |
| Regular Season \| **ALABAMA** | **74** |
| LSU Feature \| **COACH ED ORGERON** | **82** |
| Regular Season \| **MISSISSIPPI** | **86** |
| Regular Season \| **ARKANSAS** | **92** |
| Regular Season \| **TEXAS** | **98** |
| LSU Feature \| **JOE BURROW-HEISMAN TROPHY** | **104** |
| SEC Championship \| **GEORGIA** | **110** |
| Peach Bowl \| **OKLAHOMA** | **118** |
| **LSU TIGERS ROSTER** | **128** |

# INTRODUCTION

It's great to be a LSU Tiger. 2019 National Champions. What a feeling!

Led by their Heisman Trophy winning quarterback Joe Burrow, this LSU Tigers team has had quite the storybook season. The perseverance, teamwork and will to win that made up the DNA of this Tigers team was on full display week after week resulting in a season of highlights.

And when the final chapter was written, the Tigers stood on the podium in the Mercedes-Benz Superdome in New Orleans and hoisted the National Championship trophy, 42-25 winners over the Clemson Tigers.

Of course, like many seasons in the past decade, LSU fans seemed to have a singular focus entering the Tigers' 2019 campaign: "Can we beat Bama?"

Prior to traveling to Tuscaloosa, Alabama, LSU squeaked by then-No. 9 Auburn, 23-20 to set up the Game of the Century — No. 1 vs. No. 2.

The stage couldn't have been bigger. With President Donald Trump in attendance, the Tigers rolled up the most points scored by an Alabama opponent in regulation in the 90-year history of Bryant-Denny Stadium — in a 46-41 triumph.

LSU ended an eight-game losing streak against the Crimson Tide. The national coming out party solidified the Tigers' return as a national title contender and vaulted quarterback Joe Burrow to the top of the Heisman Trophy race.

There was no letdown, either.

LSU proceeded to score at least 50 points in their next three SEC romps (at Ole Miss, vs. Arkansas and Texas A&M) and finished off a perfect regular season with a 37-10 beatdown of No. 4 Georgia in the SEC Championship Game.

At 12-0, the Tigers earned the No. 1 seed in their first ever appearance in the College Football Playoff.

"It's just a good time at LSU, and everybody is pulling the same side of the rope," LSU head coach Ed Orgeron said following the SEC Championship Game. "I'm just happy for the people. I'm just happy for the players. I'm happy for the state of Louisiana and happy for LSU. This is what I'm supposed to do. I'm supposed to recruit great players and win big-time games."

Mission accomplished Coach.

LSU defeated an incredible seven teams ranked in the top 10 at the time of their matchup on their way to the national championship.

"No question, the regular season made us battle-tested," Orgeron said. "We blocked out the noise. These guys were focused."

The sport's postseason awards accurately reflect LSU's incredible season.

Burrow won the Heisman in a record-setting landslide. The most prestigious individual award in college football joined a laundry list of honors — AP National Player of the Year, Maxwell Award, Walter Camp Award, Davey O'Brien Award, Johnny Unitas Golden Arm Award — for the second-year transfer from Ohio State.

"It means so much to me — but not just me — also to LSU and to the state of Louisiana," Burrow said. "I do it for them."

The Ohio native's dominance in 2019 was unexpected. In 2018, Burrow tossed 16 touchdowns and compiled less than 2,900 passing yards. This season, Burrow averaged four touchdown passes per game (55 total) and passed for more than 5,000 yards.

"The best thing about Joe is he's a team player," Orgeron said. "All he wants to do is

Tigers quarterback Joe Burrow (9) holds the championship trophy. TODD KIRKLAND-ICON SPORTSWIRE / AP PHOTO

win. Individual awards are not high on his list.

"This is his team, and the reason it's his team is because he earned his teammate's respect. I've got to give it to Joe ... he's kind of a quiet kid, doesn't say much. He leads by his actions. But every once in a while, he'll say something when things aren't going right, and that's the mark of a true leader. And then he backs it up on the field. The whole team, everybody in the organization believes in Joe."

Burrow was far from a one-man show. Running back Clyde Edwards-Helaire and wide receivers Ja'Marr Chase and Justin Jefferson have all been instrumental in leading one of the best offenses in college football history. LSU became the first team ever to have a 5,000-yard passer, a 1,000-yard rusher and two 1,000-yard receivers, all in the same season. Chase and Jefferson also broke the school record for touchdowns with 18 each.

LSU's haul at the College Football Awards included the Jim Thorpe Award (Grant Delpit, nation's top defensive back), the Biletnikoff Award (Ja'Marr Chase, nation's top receiver) and National Coach of the Year (Ed Orgeron).

It wasn't long ago when LSU would routinely get mocked for their offense. The Tigers have won their share of games — including two national championships — in the past two decades, but couldn't shake jokes about "3 yards and a cloud of dust" and descriptors like "prehistoric."

In the blink of an eye that all changed. Other programs are scurrying to steal personnel from LSU's offensive juggernaut — including Joe Brady (passing game coordinator) — and Burrow is projected to be the No. 1 pick in the 2020 NFL Draft.

"The first season with the spread offense and having Joe run it, then having Joe Brady and Steve Ensminger here and to see the evolution of the spread offense, which our fans have been wanting for a long time," Orgeron said. "It is all pretty special."

Special indeed. ∎

LSU players celebrate winning the national championship.
DAVID J. PHILLIP / AP PHOTO

# LSU 42, CLEMSON 25

JANUARY 13, 2020 | NEW ORLEANS, LOUISIANA

## National Champions!

Burrow throws 5 TDs to rally LSU

When Joe Burrow showed up on Louisiana State's campus less than two years ago, wooed by a crawfish dinner, the irresistible charms of Coach Ed Orgeron and the opportunity to chase a dream that had been denied him at Ohio State, it was a marriage of convenience.

The gravel-throated coach needed a quarterback he'd never had before, and the baby-faced quarterback needed a team to lead after sitting on the bench for three years in his home state.

The leap of faith each took for the other came to a spectacular conclusion on Monday night, when L.S.U. capped a magical season with a 42-25 victory over Clemson to win the national championship at the Superdome.

L.S.U. did it largely by riding Burrow, who won the Heisman Trophy last month and played to that standard on Monday, using his precise right arm, his nimble legs and his keen football mind to thwart a determined Clemson defense that had been the toughest to score against in the nation this season.

Clemson battered Burrow, sacking him five times, but he nevertheless torched the opposing defenders for 463 yards passing and five touchdowns, as L.S.U. rallied from an early 10-point deficit.

The victory, which snapped Clemson's winning streak at 29 games, capped one of the most rigorous unbeaten runs any team has ever made. L.S.U. beat six teams that were among the top 13 in the final regular-season College Football Playoff rankings.

Though Clemson was trying to win its third championship in four seasons, Coach Dabo Swinney was well justified this time in playing his familiar lil' ol' Clemson card, knowing the game would be played nearly 80 miles from L.S.U.'s home stadium.

Clemson fans turned out, as they regularly do, transforming one end zone into a sea of orange. But as anyone who roamed the streets of the French Quarter in the days leading up to the game might have surmised, this was L.S.U.'s town.

"It's almost like we're in another country," Clemson linebacker Isaiah Simmons said on Saturday. "Everyone here is L.S.U. There's not really many of us."

The three previous L.S.U. national champions had all been crowned in this city, and in the 16 days since the Tigers blew out Oklahoma in the Peach Bowl, their fans had anticipated another title. The crowd, even as it waited to file in, erupted as soon as Burrow

Tigers quarterback Joe Burrow (9) reacts after throwing a touchdown during the third quarter. JONATHAN BACHMAN / GETTY IMAGES

Tigers wide receiver Ja'Marr Chase (1) beats Clemson cornerback A.J. Terrell (8) for a 52-yard first quarter touchdown reception. DAVID J. PHILLIP / AP PHOTO

**ABOVE:** Tigers wide receiver Ja'Marr Chase (1) celebrates with teammate Justin Jefferson (2) after scoring a first quarter touchdown.
GERALD HEBERT / AP PHOTO

**OPPOSITE:** Clemson quarterback Trevor Lawrence passes under pressure from Tigers linebacker K'Lavon Chaisson during first half action.
DAVID J. PHILLIP / AP PHOTO

came out of the tunnel about 90 minutes before kickoff to warm up, followed by chants of "L-S-U."

Once the ball was kicked off, with President Trump in attendance, Clemson saw to it that the home-state crowd squirmed in the stands for a little while.

Clemson surged to a 17-7 lead — the largest deficit L.S.U. had faced all season.

But no previous opponents had come close to slowing down the L.S.U. offense, which led the nation in scoring.

Burrow got L.S.U. back on track — not so much with his arm as with his feet.

While Clemson defensive coordinator Brent Venables used blitzes to bother Burrow when he set up to pass, L.S.U. offensive coordinator Steve Ensminger countered in critical situations with quarterback draws.

Burrow found a crease on third-and-goal to dash 3 yards to bring L.S.U. within 17-14, then ran away from Simmons — the star linebacker — to pick up a first down on a drive that would put L.S.U. ahead for good by dropping a 14-yard pass into the hands of Ja'Marr Chase in the back of the end zone.

And finally, out of timeouts and facing a third-and-10 at the Clemson 35 with 21 seconds left, Burrow took the snap, read the block of center Lloyd Cushenberry III and dashed 29 yards to the Clemson 6 with 14 seconds left. On the next play, Burrow hit tight end Thaddeus Moss wide open in the end zone just as he was leveled by a blitzing linebacker, James Skalski.

The touchdown, with 10 seconds left in the half, was doubly crushing.

The drive had been kept alive when

cornerback Derion Kendrick was flagged for interfering with Terrace Marshall Jr. on third-and-19 with L.S.U. pinned at its own 21.

It was precisely the type of mistake that Clemson had repeatedly benefited from against Ohio State in rallying from a 16-point deficit in the semifinal. For the most part on Monday, Clemson was making the errors.

Clemson had another critical error midway through the third quarter: Skalski was ejected for targeting when he lowered his helmet and drilled receiver Justin Jefferson in the head.

The penalty not only aided an L.S.U. touchdown — Burrow threw a short scoring pass to Moss on the next play to put his team ahead, 35-25 — it also deprived Clemson of its defensive bellwether. Swinney wrapped an arm around Skalski and offered a few words before the linebacker headed to the locker room.

After the L.S.U. defense earned another stop, Burrow went to work again, depositing a pass just where Marshall could leap to catch it in the end zone. The reception, with 12:08 to play, did not end the game — but it surely felt as if that was what happened.

The crowd roared moments later when a few strains of the L.S.U. anthem — Garth Brooks's "Calling Baton Rouge" — was played. Shortly after, Burrow sat on the bench, a smile on his face and waved an arm up and down — mimicking the student section's singular cheer. The students then followed suit, Burrow once again leading the way. ∎

Tigers quarterback Joe Burrow drags Clemson safety Denzel Johnson (14) across the goal line on his 3-yard second quarter touchdown run. KEN MURRAY-ICON SPORTSWIRE / AP PHOTO

Tigers tight end Thaddeus Moss scores a touchdown past Clemson cornerback Derion Kendrick during the third quarter. SUE OGROCKI / AP PHOTO

Head Coach Ed Orgeron hoists the National Championship trophy as his players cheer him on.
KEN MURRAY-ICON SPORTSWIRE / AP PHOTO

# LSU 55, GEORGIA SOUTHERN 3
AUGUST 31, 2019 | BATON ROUGE, LOUISIANA

# Overmatched

## Burrow, No. 6 LSU trounce Georgia Southern

LSU quarterback Joe Burrow smiled playfully while urging reporters crowding around him to write that the Tigers' new offense "showed everything we got—all of it," in its opener against overmatched Georgia Southern.

Burrow knew no one would believe him—not with LSU's first true test coming up next weekend at No. 10 Texas. Yet, even the plays LSU did run will put the rest of their opponents on notice that the Tigers are transformed offensively.

Burrow tied an LSU single-game record with five touchdown passes before halftime and the Tigers held a multi-touchdown lead for all but the first six minutes in a 55-3 victory on Saturday night.

Unleashing a new spread scheme, the Tigers (1-0) scored 21 points in the first quarter something they never did in any quarter last season. Their point total was the most in a non-overtime game since scoring 63 against New Mexico State in 2014.

"I wanted 60 tonight," Burrow said. "We've definitely come out of the stone age."

Directing his unit with pace and precision, Burrow completed 23 of 27 passes for 278 yards without an interception before being subbed out after LSU's first possession of the second half, which ended with a field goal. That was Burrow's last chance to break the LSU mark of five touchdowns in a game set by Zach Mettenberger in 2013.

Designed largely by new passing-game coordinator Joe Brady and overseen by incumbent offensive coordinator Steve Ensminger, the up-tempo, no-huddle scheme routinely features five receiving targets, some of whom give Burrow the option to unload the ball quickly if under pressure.

"We're going to run the spread offense. We're going to score points. We've got athletes. That's what we do," coach Ed Orgeron said. "The scheme is a lot better this year. We have answers to different coverages."

Burrow often was ready for the snap—and could be seen hopping anxiously—while officials stood over center, forcing the Tigers to wait until the Eagles (0-1) had a chance to make substitutions.

"I got on the officials a couple of times because we didn't sub, and they were holding the ball up. We are trying to go tempo," Burrow said. "We are going to keep building on this thing and make it even better."

Burrow's first touchdown pass capped a 75-yard drive that took just 2:24 off the clock. LSU led 14-0 with 8:10 remaining in the

Georgia Southern wide receiver Mills Ridings (5) is swarmed by the LSU defense. MARIANNA MASSEY / GETTY IMAGES

opening period. None of the Tigers' six touchdown drives directed by Burrow lasted longer than 3:50.

Burrow completed passes to nine players. By the end, 14 LSU players had caught a pass, led by Justin Jefferson's five catches for 87 yards and a touchdown.

Terrace Marshall Jr. caught three short scoring passes.

Tight end Thaddeus Moss, the son of Hall-of-Fame receiver Randy Moss, caught two passes for 61 yards, including a 44-yarder deep down the right side.

"It was a blast," Moss said. "Our offense has been the talk of the off-season. It felt good to finally put that out there."

Georgia Southern, which won 10 games last season, was confronted with an LSU defense prepared to stop its triple-option. Eagles starting quarterback Shai Werts completed one pass for no yards and was held to minus-7 yards rushing before being knocked out of the game with an apparent upper body injury in the first half.

"Obviously we ran into a really good football team," Georgia Southern coach Chad Lunsford said. "Coach O came across the field and said, `Hey, we've been preparing for you guys since February,' and that showed."

LSU finished with a 472-98 advantage in total yards. ■

Tight end Thaddeus Moss (81) and guard Damien Lewis (68) signal a touchdown by Tigers running back Clyde Edwards-Helaire (22). ANDY ALTENBURGER-ICON SPORTSWIRE / AP PHOTO

# LSU 45, TEXAS 38

SEPTEMBER 7, 2019 | AUSTIN, TEXAS

# Texas Shootout

## Burrow's 4 TD passes lead LSU over Texas

Joe Burrow was nearly perfect in the second half against Texas.

He had to be.

With Longhorns quarterback Sam Ehlinger matching him nearly blow for blow, Burrow and No. 6 LSU's new, wide-open offense could afford to make no mistakes. They didn't, and Burrow delivered all the big throws for the Tigers in a wild 45-38 win over the No. 9 Longhorns Saturday night in one of the biggest nonconference matchups of the season.

Burrow passed for 471 yards and four touchdowns, the last one to Justin Jefferson for 61 yards with 2:27 to play in a game that saw Texas storm back from a 20-7 halftime deficit and the teams trade seven touchdowns in the second half.

"Man, Joe was so fired up," LSU coach Ed Orgeron said. "The kid is a baller. He lives for that moment and I'll tell you what, those were some tough plays"

Burrow was razor sharp after halftime when he was 15-of-18 passing for 251 yards and two touchdowns. The final touchdown to Jefferson came on a third-and-long when Burrow stepped up to avoid a blitz and fired the pass. The completion was good enough for a first down and Jefferson did the rest when he broke a tackle and burst up the sideline to the end zone.

"I think if they get the ball back, it would have been a different story," said Orgeron, who was watching Ehlinger riddle the Tigers defense. "A phenomenal call, a phenomenal catch, a phenomenal play."

Jefferson finished with three touchdown catches and was one of three LSU receivers with more than 100 yards.

"They (Texas) were playing so well, I told the guys, we gotta get 40 and we'll win," Burrow said. "We had over 500 yards. It could have been 600, 700."

The touchdown put LSU (2-0) up by 14 but Ehlinger brought Texas back again with his fourth touchdown pass and second on the night to Devin Duvernay. LSU didn't put the game away until Texas came within inches of recovering an onside kick with 22 seconds left.

Ehlinger finished with 401 yards passing and four touchdowns for the Longhorns (1-1).

The win will give LSU some big early momentum in the long-term goal of reaching the College Football Playoff, but the rough SEC schedule still looms.

Tigers WR Ja'Marr Chase (1) out leaps the Longhorns Jalen Green (3) to haul in a pass. JOHN RIVERA-ICON SPORTSWIRE / AP PHOTO

LSU cornerback Derek Stingley Jr., left, breaks up a pass intended for Texas wide receiver Collin Johnson during the first half. ERIC GAY / AP PHOTO

**ABOVE:** Tigers wide receiver Terrace Marshall Jr. (6) scores on a 26-yard touchdown pass early in the fourth quarter. MO KHURSHEED- TVF MEDIA / AP PHOTO

**OPPOSITE:** Burrow prepares to receive the snap during second half action. ROBERT BACKMAN-CAL SPORT MEDIA / AP PHOTO

"I think it's a big statement, but obviously we want to play better," Orgeron said.

Texas coach Tom Herman said he'll immediately get his team to focus on the Big 12.

"This is Game 2 of a marathon," Herman said. "All our goals are still out there."

After the game, Herman and Burrow had a long embrace on the field. Herman was an assistant at Ohio State when he recruited Burrow to the Buckeyes but then left to take the head coaching job at Houston. Burrow spent three years at Ohio State before transferring to LSU.

Burrow also made a point to talk with Ehlinger, who kept bringing Texas back.

"He's a super tough guy. I was honored to be on the same field with him," Burrow said.

Kickoff temperatures were hovering around 100 degrees and LSU players had trouble with cramps all night. The cramps often seemed to hit just as Texas drives were gaining momentum. The home crowd booed when it thought an LSU player was stalling. Texas players didn't seem to have the same cramping problems.

Herman was asked if LSU's cramping halted his team's momentum.

"Yes," he said.

When asked if he thought LSU players were doing it on purpose, "I have no idea." ■

Tigers safety Marcel Brooks (9) sacks Texas quarterback Sam Ehlinger (11).
RIC TAPIA / AP PHOTO

# LSU 65, NORTHWESTERN STATE 14

SEPTEMBER 14, 2019 | BATON ROUGE, LOUISIANA

# The Joe Show

## Burrow clinical, No. 4 LSU downs Northwestern State

LSU coach Ed Orgeron had to play starting quarterback Joe Burrow longer than planned after a more competitive first half than expected against Northwestern State.

So Burrow seized the opportunity to post another impressive statistical line that will only help his cause if he winds up in the running for the Heisman Trophy.

Burrow completed 21 of 24 passes for 373 yards and two touchdowns, and fourth-ranked LSU pulled away in the second half for a 65-14 victory Saturday night.

"This is who we are as an offense," Burrow said. "We are going to take our quick passes and our deep shots and that is going to continue to work well for us."

For the second time in LSU's first three games, Burrow was subbed out in the third quarter because of a lopsided score. He is now 75 of 90 (83.3 percent) passing for 1,122 yards and 11 touchdowns this season.

Burrow also ran for 30 yards and a touchdown against Northwestern State (0-3), an FCS team that surprisingly kept the game close until the Tigers (3-0) dominated the third quarter.

"I felt confident that we were going to go out there and just keep chopping away," Orgeron said. "I didn't raise my voice that much at halftime.

"When you win like that ... I'm not going to complain at all," Orgeron added.

In leading LSU to the 800th victory in the program's 126-year history, Burrow also became just the school's sixth quarterback to throw for 300 or more yards in consecutive games. Only Rohan Davey did it in three straight games, a mark Burrow can match next weekend.

Both of Burrow's TD tosses went to sophomore Terrace Marshall Jr., who has six touchdown catches this season after none last season. Marshall's first touchdown was an opportunistic, diving grab of a ball that missed its intended target when tight end Stephen Sullivan stumbled.

The Tigers' Clyde Edwards-Helaire and Tyrion Davis-Price each ran for two TDs and John Emery had one, while Justin Jefferson caught five passes for 124 yards. LSU's Trey Palmer added a 54-yard punt return touchdown in the fourth quarter.

"I'm happy with the point output, but I still feel like we could have done better," Burrow said.

LSU players heard some boos when first half ended with the Tigers up 24-14.

Having lost 33-7 at home to Division II Midwestern State a week earlier, the Demons were not expected to enjoy much success

Tigers linebacker Patrick Queen (8) prepares to blitz the quarterback. JOHN KORDUNER-ICON SPORTSWIRE / AP PHOTO

against a Tigers squad coming off a victory at Texas. But they took a 7-3 lead when Eppler fired a 17-yard scoring pass to Shorts in the first quarter—the first TD Northwestern State had ever scored against LSU in 12 meetings dating back to 1911.

The Tigers responded with consecutive touchdown drives. But Northwestern State came back with a six-play, 75-yard scoring drive, which ended with Fitzwater uncovered in the end zone after outside linebacker Andre Anthony lost track of the tight end.

LSU went back up 10 on Edwards-Helaire's second short TD run, but the Tigers' chance to widen the lead before halftime took a hit when Dylan Wilson intercepted one of only two of Burrow's passes all half that did not find a receiver. Northwestern State took over at the LSU 17, but was held to a missed field goal.

"We had the opportunity to cut it to three or seven," Demons coach Brad Laird said. "Moving forward against a good football team, you've got to take advantage of that. But I'm really excited about the effort from my guys."

At halftime, Burrow said, "We were all pretty disappointed in ourselves."

The Tigers turned up the intensity afterward, scoring on their next four possessions while holding the Demons without a first down on their first three series of the third quarter. ∎

Tigers running back Clyde Edwards-Helaire (22) breaks into the open past Northwestern State outside linebacker Landon King (32) during first half action. PATRICK DENNIS / AP PHOTO

*"That's all that's ever mattered to me: winning games. When my stats weren't great last year, and we were winning games, I said the same thing. I'll say the same thing this year."*
—Joe Burrow

# The Difference-Maker
## QB Joe Burrow Sets the Tone for LSU

He is one tough S.O.B.

"You have no idea," says LSU safety Grant Delpit.

Try me.

"So we're in spring practice," Delpit begins, and he stops and smiles at the thought of his tough-guy story about Tigers quarterback Joe Burrow.

But something doesn't feel right.

"He got hit, he thought late, on a play," Delpit continues. "They call [quarterback] run on the next play, he comes around the end and he goes right after the guy he thinks hit him. Running right at him, and the next thing you know, we're all fighting, offense and defense."

Who hit him?

"I think," Delpit laughs, "he thought it was me."

It doesn't matter who you are. An opposing defender, a teammate in practice, a projected top-six pick in next year's NFL draft, like Delpit.

Joe Burrow is coming. Get out of the way.

"There was a little fight after I got hit late that first time, but I wasn't part of it," Burrow explains, and he's starting to get lathered up right now just thinking about it. "So, yeah, I gotta start another fight. Next play, I started another one. I have no idea how long it lasted. But we were getting after it."

Said Delpit: "Man, I love that guy."

That, more than anything, is why we're where we are today, with a loaded LSU team rolling into the national championship game with a tough-guy quarterback who has changed the way they think and act.

We barely heard from LSU this offseason. No problems, no drama. None of those questions of what could be from seasons past.

All those years of everything in place except the quarterback, all those wasted seasons with all that NFL talent—only to come up short while chasing Alabama in the SEC. And all that changed with the addition of one tough and talented player in the spring of 2018.

Just how important was it when Burrow, the hardscrabble grinder from Athens County, Ohio, found his way to the South and caught on with a program desperate for real, genuine attitude?

"He saved our ass," says LSU head coach Ed Orgeron.

Burrow hears Orgeron's words, and his head drops. He has just returned from a trip to Athens, where so many live below the poverty line and have never made it out. A place that can swallow hope.

He sat for three years at Ohio State, backing up Braxton Miller and J.T. Barrett and Cardale Jones. Dwayne Haskins was next in line when Burrow finally bailed.

He never wanted to go home to Athens during those three years at Ohio State, because he'd only hear the inevitable: Even he, a kid from a proud football family, was swallowed. May as well come back home.

Now he's nervously rubbing a big oak table in the LSU football offices, and the toughest guy in college football is about to reveal a side few see.

"I didn't save them," he says, his eyes

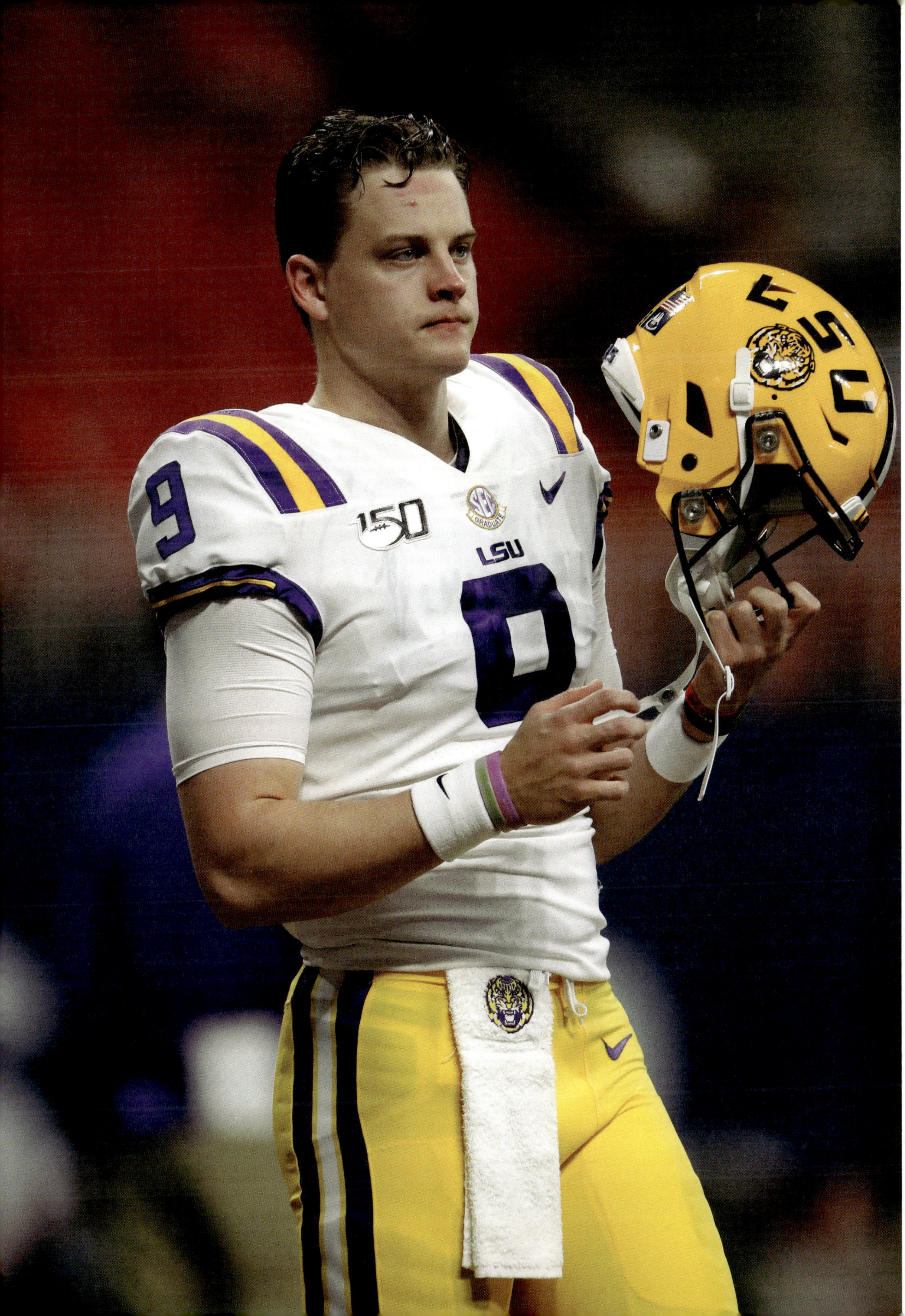
150
LSU

beginning to well. "They saved me."

The momentary silence is overwhelming.

"Without Coach O, without him believing in me, who knows, I might have gone to Cincinnati and lost the job," Burrow says. "I might have gone to North Carolina and lost the job and not be playing.

"Now we're getting ready to make a run at this thing, the whole thing, and who knows what will happen with my career after this."

\*\*\*

He knew it was a bad throw in last year's Fiesta Bowl as soon as it left his hand. What he didn't know as he tried to run down UCF cornerback Brandon Moore to rectify his mistake was that defensive tackle Joey Connors was zeroing in on him.

Connors took Burrow down with a blindside hit. A dirty hit. Burrow was decleated and driven into the ground. Moore turned the poor throw into a 93-yard touchdown return, and suddenly, LSU was down 14-3 early, looking like it might be the latest Power Five team taken down in a major bowl by giant killer UCF.

On the sideline, Orgeron screamed at his offensive staff to get backup quarterback Myles Brennan ready to play. Burrow slowly pulled himself off the turf, walked to the sideline and got in Orgeron's face.

"You're not taking me out of this game!" he screamed.

Then he went out and completed 19 of his next 28 passes for 363 yards and four touchdowns—and no more interceptions—and a depleted LSU team beat UCF and wrapped up its first 10-win season since 2013.

"We put two full IV bags in him after the game," Orgeron says. "He's not one of those fake tough guys. He walks it every day."

When Burrow was leaving Ohio State, he chose LSU because he wanted to play in the SEC and he wanted a program that needed him.

He knew about the shaky history of LSU quarterbacks since the national championship season of 2007 (no All-SEC selections, 84 INTs) and knew he had to shake it up from Day 1.

He arrived in June of 2018, and his introduction to the team was set in the heart

Joe Burrow (9) celebrates with his offensive line after rushing for a touchdown. KEVIN C. COX / GETTY IMAGES

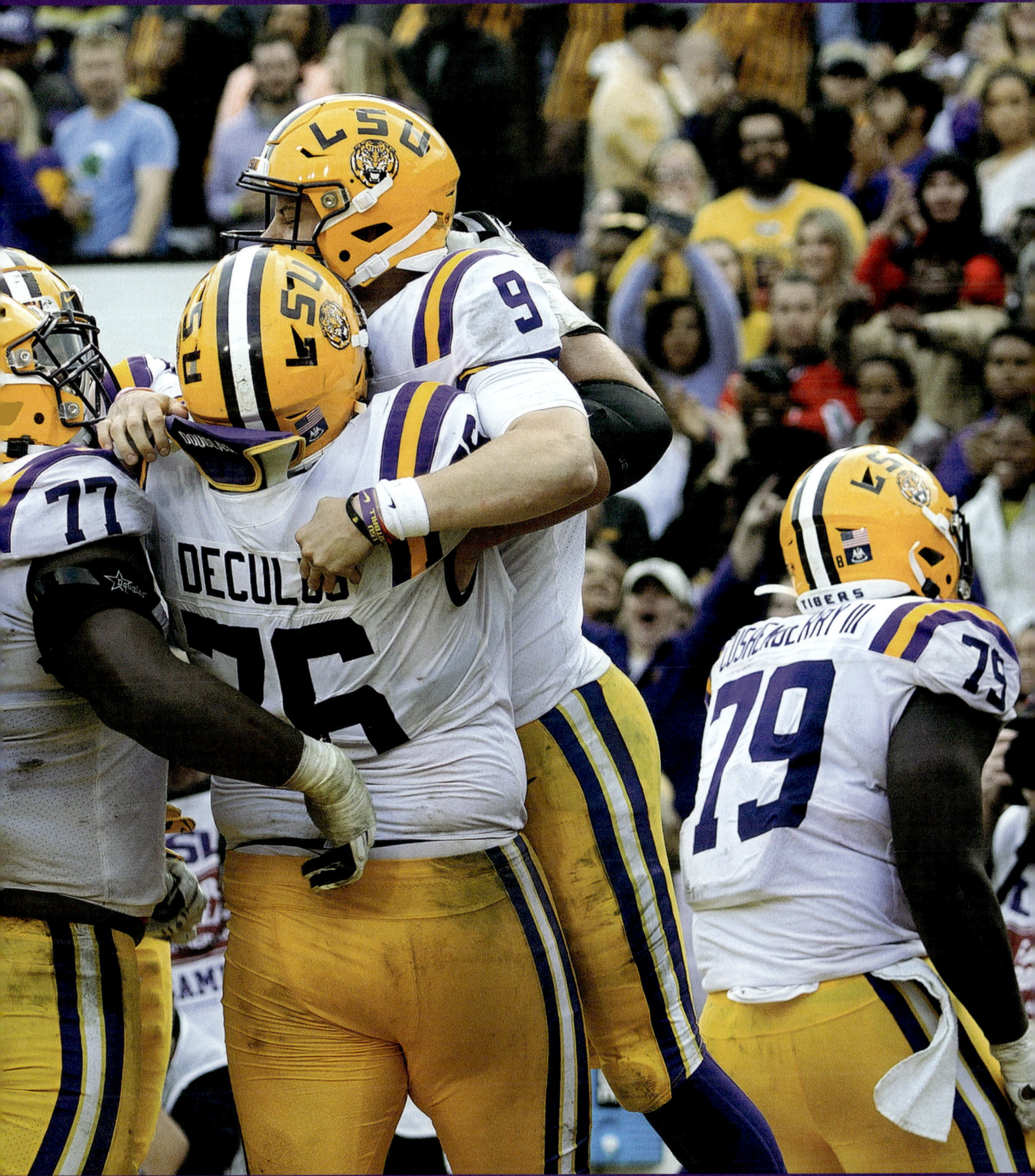
LSU
9
77
79

Burrow and wide receiver Ja'Marr Chase (1) celebrate after connecting on a touchdown pass. GERALD HEBERT / AP PHOTO

of the bayou summer: 95 degrees, 100 percent humidity. He blew away his teammates, winning nearly every conditioning test.

"I remember thinking, Who is this guy?" says LSU center Lloyd Cushenberry III. "The next thing you know, he's in the locker room, and he's hanging around the offensive linemen. You know, those quarterbacks usually stick together. Not Joe. He belongs with us."

Teammates can tell when someone on the field with them isn't genuine. More to the point, they can tell when someone is. But when you grow up around football—when your dad was a longtime successful defensive coordinator at Ohio and your brothers played at Nebraska—lacking an understanding for how to thrive within a team environment doesn't tend to be a problem.

Those who work and lead and set an example for others are those who find success.

A few months after that day in June, Burrow was picking himself off the turf in the season opener against eighth-ranked Miami and its athletic and dynamic defense and persevering in a big win over a Top 10 team. Two weeks after that, he led a game-winning drive in the final minute at No. 7 Auburn.

LSU head coach Ed Orgeron, left, celebrates with Burrow after beating UCF in the Fiesta Bowl. CHRISTIAN PETERSEN / GETTY IMAGES

The locker room after the game was a madhouse.

"That's when everyone was like, Hey, we got something here," Delpit says.

After years of the unknown and uncertainty with Jordan Jefferson and Ryan Perrilloux, and Brandon Harris and Danny Etling, and every quarterback in between, LSU finally knew what it had at the most important position on the field.

Someone who could win big.

"I didn't consciously try to be someone different," Burrow says. "A lot of coaches try to tell people what kind of leader they should be, but everybody is kind of their own leader. Tom Brady's leadership isn't the same as Matt Ryan's. Everyone has their own secret sauce. You can't steal someone else's secret sauce. If Burger King tried to make Cane's sauce, it would be crap.

"Everyone has their own. You just have to find yours."

The Tigers, too, have clearly found their secret sauce.

"It's more than their ability to throw the ball consistently now," says one SEC coach. "It's Burrows' attitude; they're feeding off it. He has made them the most dangerous team in the league." ■

# LSU 66, VANDERBILT 38

SEPTEMBER 21, 2019 | NASHVILLE, TENNESSEE

## The Beat Goes On

### Burrow slings LSU-record 6 TDs in rout of Vandy

LSU always has played stingy defense. Now the Tigers have a high-octane offense and no plans at all to slow down anytime soon.

"Score, be aggressive," LSU coach Ed Orgeron said. "That's our mentality. We're going to be aggressive. We're going to go get it. We're not slowing down for anything."

The Tigers' aggressive approach paid off Saturday as Joe Burrow tossed four of his school-record six touchdown passes to Ja'Marr Chase and threw for 398 yards, leading No. 4 LSU to a 66-38 romp over Vanderbilt.

"They told me when it happened," Burrow said of his TD record. "I was more focused on going to get another one."

LSU (4-0, 1-0 Southeastern Conference) beat Vanderbilt (0-3, 0-2) for the eighth consecutive time. This marked the first meeting between these SEC charter members since 2010.

The Tigers scored their most points this season and most ever in regulation against an SEC opponent. The 104 combined points tied South Carolina's 65-39 victory over Mississippi State in 1995 for the fourth-highest scoring total in an SEC game that didn't go into overtime.

"We heard on the pregame (shows) that we were one-dimensional," said LSU center Lloyd Cushenberry III. "So we had to prove them wrong."

They needed 2 minutes, 11 seconds, or less on each of their first seven scoring drives. LSU also scored 4 seconds after Micah Baskerville returned an onside kick 46 yards to open the third quarter on Burrow's fifth TD pass.

Baskerville later blocked a punt he recovered for a score.

Burrow had a game for the record books.

He became both the first LSU quarterback to throw for 350 yards or more in three consecutive games. His 357 yards passing by halftime also was the most in school history.

Burrow hit 13 of his first 14 passes for 244 yards before throwing his second incompletion at 9:19 in the second quarter. He finished 25-of-34 and left the game early in the fourth quarter.

"I think we're starting to see that we can do this every game against every team," Burrow said. "This is who we are as an offense. We're gonna go try to score every time, we're gonna throw the ball around. And we're going to throw it to open up the run. So I'm happy with where we are right now.

"But you always like to get better."

"It's good," Orgeron said. "I think that there's more to come. I really do. I think Joe is a fantastic player. He has a fantastic coach in [offensive coordinator] Steve Ensminger. We have a great plan, and as long as we protect

Tigers wide receiver Ja'Marr Chase (1) flexes after making a tough catch. ANDY ALTENBURGER-ICON SPORTSWIRE / AP PHOTO

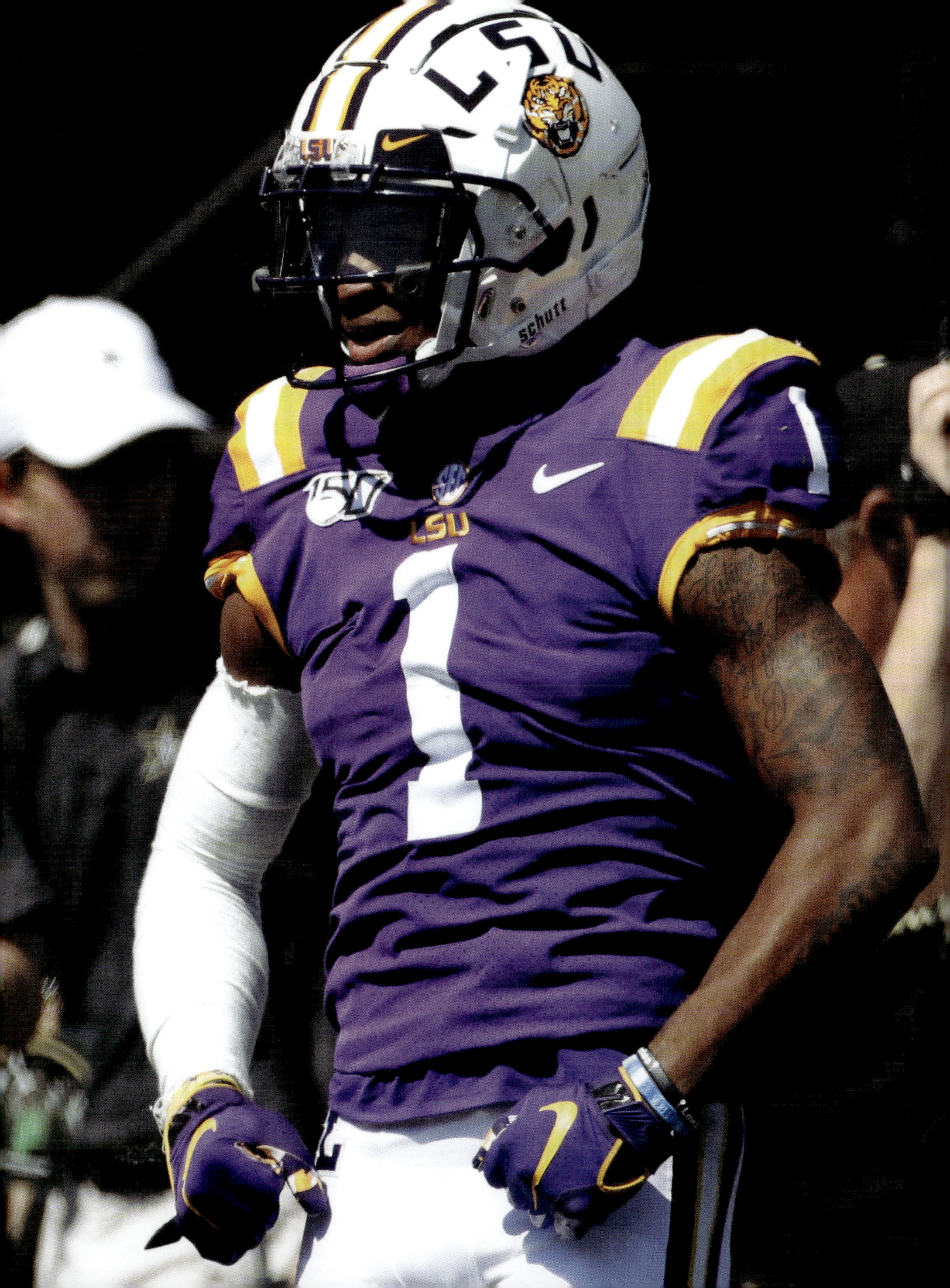
LSU
schutt
LSU
1

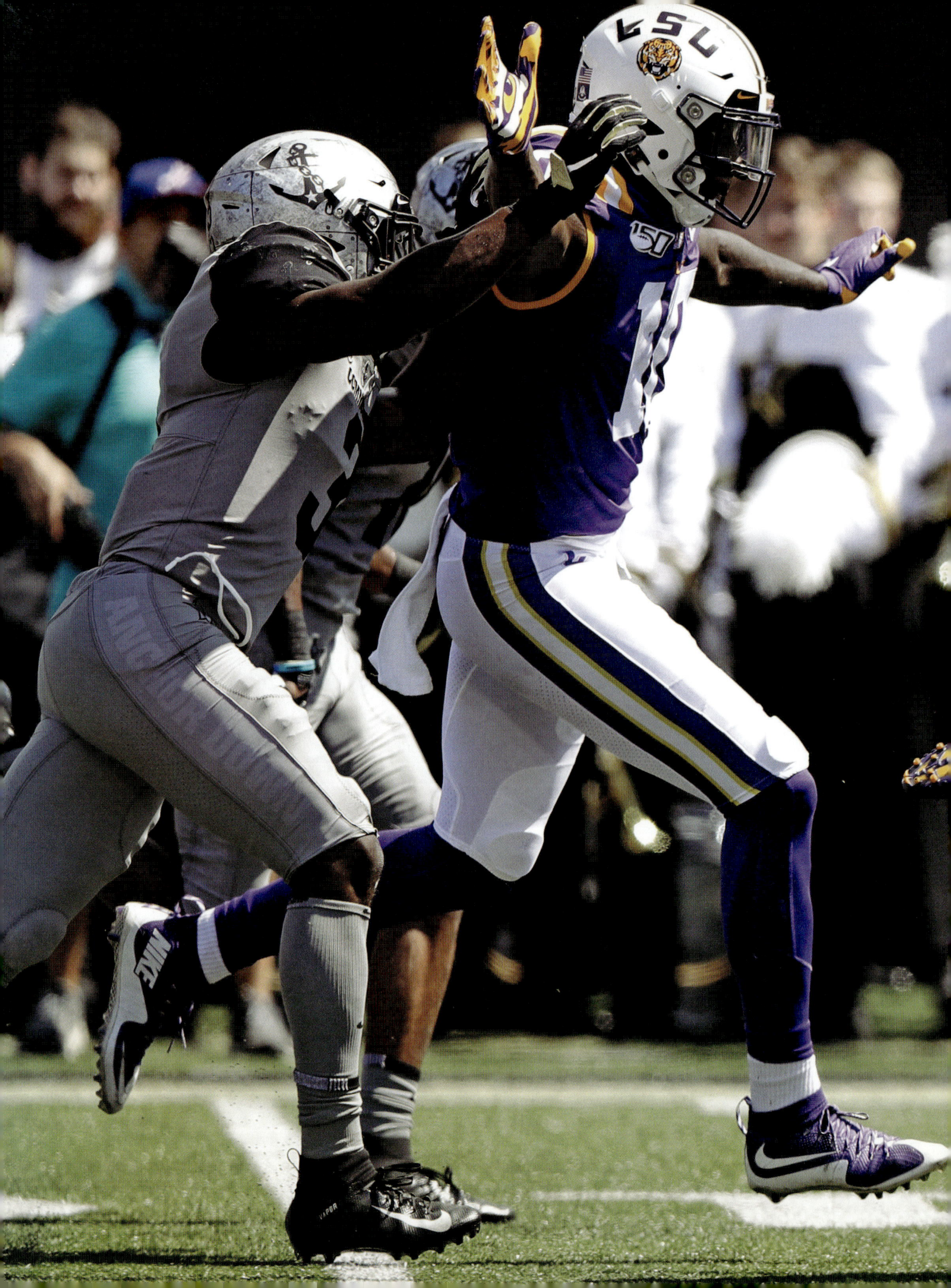

Tigers tight end Stephen Sullivan (10) screens off two Vanderbilt defenders as teammate Ja'Marr Chase (1) races to the end zone on a 51-yard touchdown pass during the first half.
MARK HUMPHREY / AP PHOTO

the quarterback we're going to make big plays here at LSU."

And Burrow kept throwing to Chase. The sophomore caught TDs of 64, 25 and 51 yards in the first quarter and adding a 16-yarder in the third. He finished with 10 receptions for 229 yards, most by an LSU receiver since Odell Beckham Jr. had 204 against Furman in 2013.

"I'm just happy I played today," Chase said after not seeing the field against Northwestern State last week in a coach's decision.

Chase entered the day tied for third in touchdown catches with just one, well behind Justin Jefferson's four and Terrace Marshall Jr.'s six. The three have a season-long bet on who will finish with the most scores, and the winner gets his choice of Waffle House or $100.

"We've got a lot of bets going on with me and Terrace and Justin," Chase said. "I had to score at least three today so I could be back in the touchdown race."

Vanderbilt had never before played two of the nation's top five teams within the first three weeks of a season. At least the Commodores scored on their first drive, which they didn't manage in an opening defeat to No. 3 Georgia or a loss at Purdue. They scored their most points yet this season but had two turnovers.

"We were playing with house money, man," Vanderbilt coach Derek Mason said. "We had a chance to really take some chances, try to force some things to happen. Those things didn't necessarily go our way." ∎

Quarterback Joe Burrow (9) throws one of his six touchdowns on the day.
MARK HUMPHREY / AP PHOTO

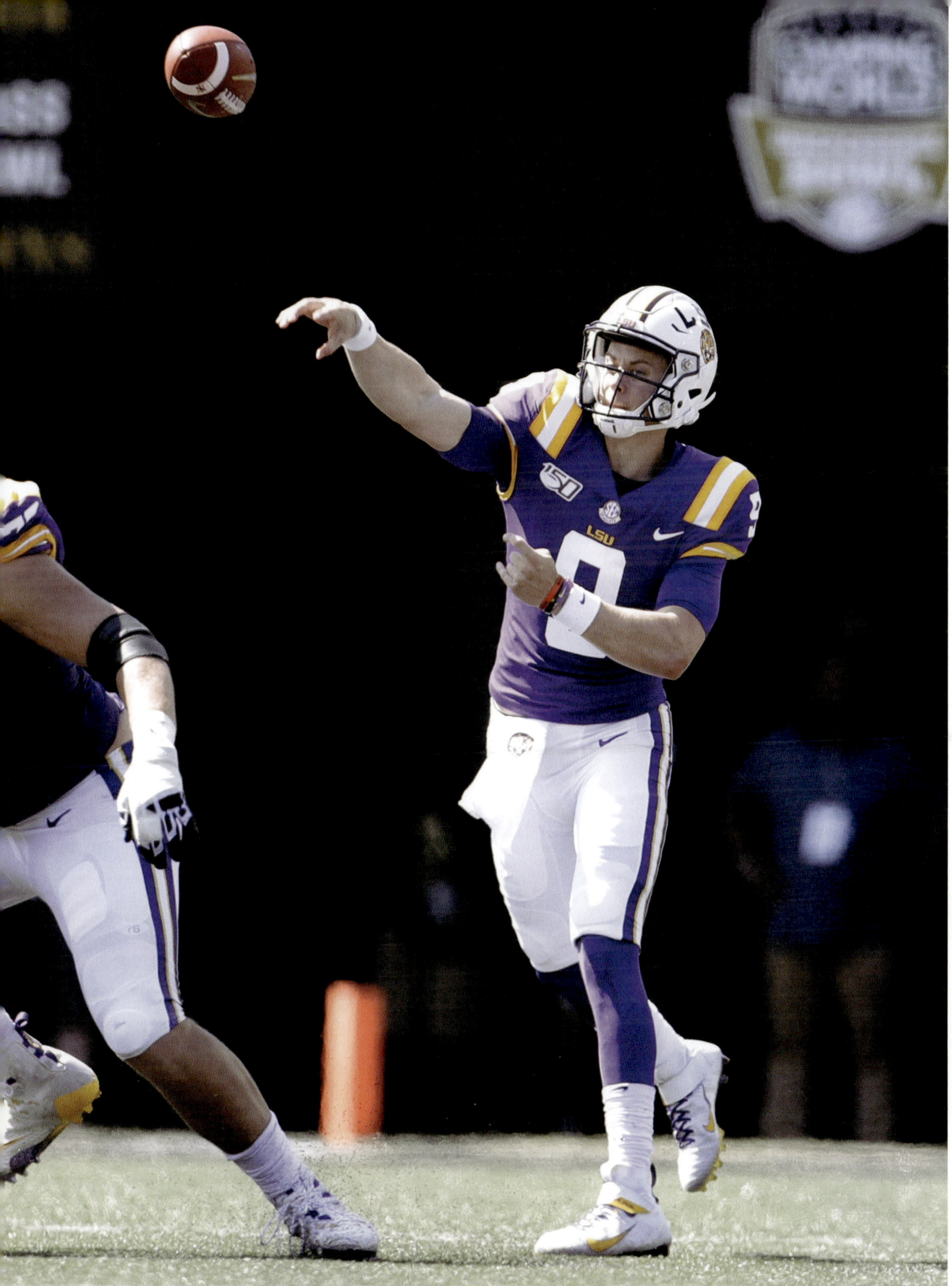

# LSU 42, UTAH STATE 6
OCTOBER 5, 2019 | BATON ROUGE, LOUISIANA

# Bayou Blowout
## Joe Burrow makes history as No. 5 LSU routs Utah State

Joe Burrow didn't sound too impressed with his latest historically significant performance for unbeaten LSU.

Burrow became the first LSU quarterback to eclipse 300 yards passing in four straight games and threw for five touchdowns to help the fifth-ranked Tigers defeat Utah State 42-6 on Saturday.

"Last year, we would have been very happy" with a 36-point victory margin and 601 yards of offense, Burrow said. "But this is a new team and a new offense. Things have changed around here when you are not happy with this performance."

Perhaps that's a wise stance considering what's coming up on the Tigers' schedule. Three of their next four games are against teams that spent the past week ranked in the top 10: No. 10 Florida, No. 7 Auburn and No. 1 Alabama.

Burrow, who has finished only one fourth quarter this season because of lopsided scores, has completed 78.3 percent of his passes for 1,864 yards and 22 touchdowns through five games as he remains on pace to threaten most LSU single-season passing records.

He completed 27 of 38 passes for 344 yards and was intercepted once on a tipped pass against Utah State before being replaced by Myles Brennan on LSU's second series of the fourth quarter. Burrow also rushed for 42 yards and touchdown. In three games this season, Burrow has passed for at least five TDs, including his school-record six at Vanderbilt.

"Our goal is simple when we have the ball," said receiver Ja'Marr Chase, who caught his sixth touchdown pass this season. "Go out there and put on a display. It's fun out there."

Justin Jefferson caught two scoring passes for LSU (5-0). His second TD on a 39-yard throw put Burrow beyond 300 yards. Burrow's other TD strikes went to Derrick Dillon and tight end Thaddeus Moss.

LSU's defense bottled up a Utah State offense that came in averaging 533 yards 38.5 points, intercepting quarterback Jordan Love three times.

"We got stomped on offense. There you have it," Utah State coach Gary Andersen said. "Couldn't run the ball. Couldn't throw the ball. You name it, we couldn't do it."

Freshman Derek Stingley Jr. displayed veteran-like savvy when he timed a spinning leap to high-point Love's fade pass to the right pylon in front of the intended receiver for his second interception this season. The Tigers responded with a 99-yard touchdown drive.

Tigers cornerback Kary Vincent Jr. (5) celebrates with teammate Dee Anderson (11) after the Tigers defense forced a turnover.
JOHN KORDUNER-ICON SPORTSWIRE / AP PHOTO

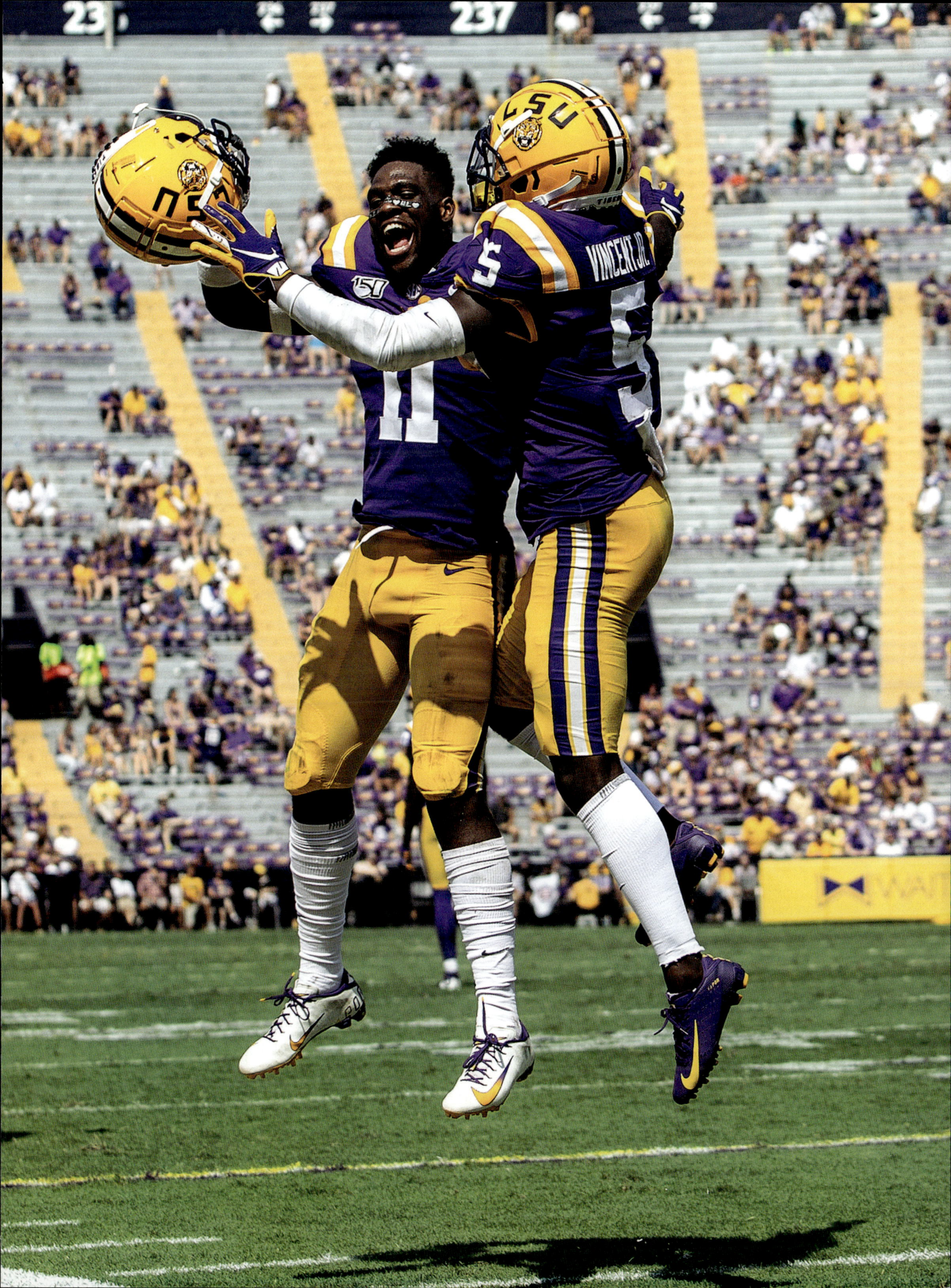
237
LSU
VINCENT JR.

**ABOVE:** Tigers wide receiver Justin Jefferson (2) makes a tough catch as Utah State cornerback Cameron Haney defends. CHRIS GRAYTHEN / GETTY IMAGES

**RIGHT:** Tigers tight end Thaddeus Moss (81) breaks the tackle of Utah State linebacker David Woodward (9) on his way to the endzone. CHRIS GRAYTHEN / GETTY IMAGES

Tigers quarterback Joe Burrow (9) passes under pressure from Utah State defensive end Tipa Galeai (10) in the first half. GERALD HEBERT / AP PHOTO

Preseason All-America safety Grant Delpit and Kary Vincent also intercepted Love, who finished 15 of 30 for 130 yards. The Aggies (3-2) totaled 159 yards of offense.

"We've been hearing a lot of noise from outside, talking about we can't tackle and stuff like that," Delpit said. "We came out and proved it today. Utah State's a great team with a great offense, and I think we played lights out on defense and can hopefully carry that into next week."

LSU's point total was a season-low, but coach Ed Orgeron noted that his offense backed off its usual torrid pace of play to help its defense make adjustments, rest and hydrate between series on a hot day against a Utah State offense that also plays fast.

"It wasn't as fun, but it worked," Orgeron said. "This game was methodical. We were chewing up clock." ∎

# LSU 42, FLORIDA 28

OCTOBER 12, 2019 | BATON ROUGE, LOUISIANA

# No Paper Tigers

Joe Burrow's 3 TDs lift No. 5 LSU over No. 7 Florida

The first thing Joe Burrow did after launching the longest — and most decisive — of his three touchdown passes against Florida was embrace a pair of offensive linemen who'd kept pass-rushers at bay all night.

Then the Tigers quarterback skipped toward the jubilant LSU bench area, fist-pumping all the way.

Burrow passed for 293 yards and led fifth-ranked LSU to three unanswered touchdowns after the Tigers had fallen behind early in the second half to emerge with a 42-28 victory over No. 7 Florida on Saturday night.

Facing a Florida defense that came in leading the nation in interceptions and leading the Southeastern Conference in sacks, the Tigers (6-0, 2-0 SEC) totaled 511 yards without giving up a sack or committing a turnover.

"We knew that last year they got after us up front. Our offensive line took that personally," Burrow said, referring to a 27-19 loss to the Gators in Gainesville, Florida. "I was just so proud of those guys. There was no pressure the entire night."

LSU coach Ed Orgeron declared that holding Florida's defense without a sack was "the biggest stat of the night," noting how the Gators' defensive ends had "destroyed" opposing offensive lines in previous games.

"I don't think we were able to get pressure on him, and when we did, he did a god job of scrambling," Florida coach Dan Mullen said of Burrow.

Ja'Marr Chase had 127 yards receiving and the second of his two touchdowns was a 54-yarder to give LSU a two-score lead with 5 minutes, 43 seconds left. Justin Jefferson caught 10 passes for 123 yards and a touchdown.

Burrow, meanwhile, went 21-of-24, meaning he had the same number of touchdown tosses and incomplete passes.

"Once we protect the quarterback, I feel confident in us moving the football," Orgeron said.

Clyde Edwards-Helaire rushed for 134 yards and two scores.

"Their ability to run the ball was a big difference," Mullen said.

The Tigers still have yet to score fewer than 42 points in a game this season.

Kyle Trask was 23-of-39 passing for 310 yards and three touchdowns for Florida (6-1, 3-1), but was done in by freshman Derek Stingley Jr.'s interception in the LSU end zone in the fourth quarter, when the Gators were trying to tie the game.

"We did a pretty good job executing all night," Mullen said. "But the margin for error in big games is really small."

Tigers nose tackle Tyler Shelvin (72) celebrates after a sack. JOHN KORDUNER·ICON SPORTSWIRE / AP PHOTO

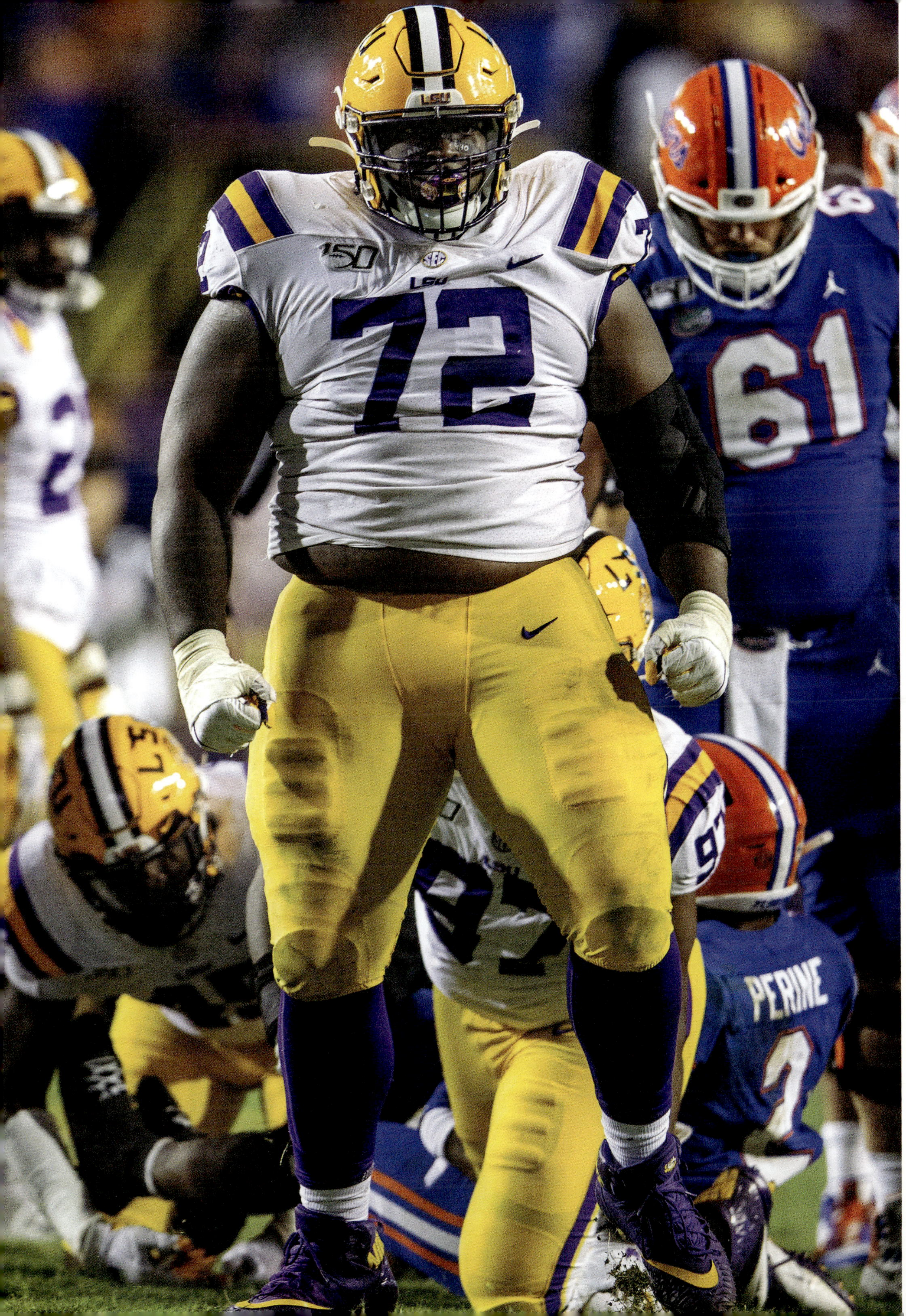
LSU
72
61
PERINE

**ABOVE:** Tigers wide receiver Justin Jefferson (2) holds on to make the catch. MARIANNA MASSEY / GETTY IMAGES

**OPPOSITE:** Florida linebacker David Reese II, left, defensive back Donovan Stiner and defensive back Trey Dean III (21) try to slow down Tigers tight end Stephen Sullivan (10) after a reception in the first half. GERALD HERBERT / AP PHOTO

Soon after, Burrow spotted Chase running free down the right sideline, and a Tiger Stadium crowd about 100,000 strong was in virtual delirium.

Florida led 28-21 after opening the second half with an eight-play, 75-yard scoring drive that ended with Van Jefferson's second touchdown catch of the game.

But LSU tied it less than four minutes later on Edwards-Helaire's 5-yard run. Tyrion Davis-Price put the Tigers back in front with a 33-yard run on LSU's next possession.

The first half was played to a 21-all tie with Florida using methodical drives to answer each of the first three touchdowns scored by LSU's high-octane attack.

LSU's first touchdown drive, capped by a 9-yard pass to Chase, took two plays and 32 seconds, starting with Edwards-Helaire's 57-yard run. The Gators responded with a 12-play drive that took more than six minutes, ending with Trask's 5-yard pass to Trevon Grimes.

After Justin Jefferson's 7-yard TD catch capped a five-play drive that covered 82 yards in just 2:09, Florida answered with a 13-play drive, ending with Emory Jones' fourth-and-goal pass under pressure to Lamical Perine, who deftly corralled the ball after it was tipped by linebacker Patrick Queen.

LSU took the lead just 1:29 later on Edwards-Helaire's 39-yard run, and Florida tied it again with an 11-play drive that finished with Van Jefferson's first touchdown on a 6-yard pass from Trask.

The Gators wound up possessing the ball for 38:19, while LSU had the ball for 21:41. But Orgeron doesn't sound inclined to slow his offense's pace to help his defense rest between possessions.

"We feel we can score, we feel we've got athletes in space and we're not going to stop," Orgeron said. ∎

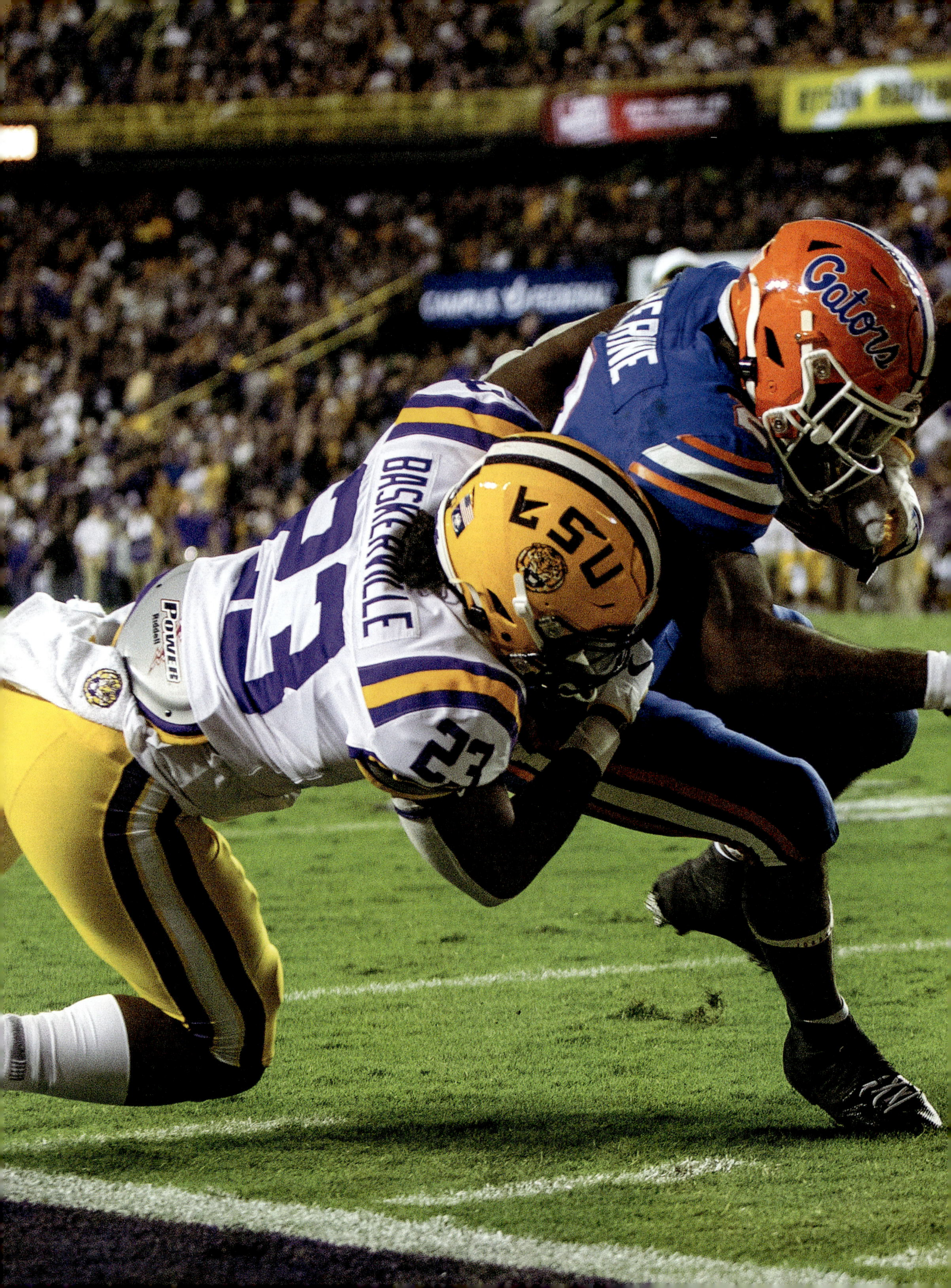
Gators
BASKERVILLE
23
LSU

Tigers safety JaCoby Stevens (3) and linebacker Micah Baskerville (23) make the touchdown saving tackle.
JOHN KORDUNER-ICON SPORTSWIRE / AP PHOTO

# Leader of the D

## Safety Grant Delpit does whatever team needs

You never know where you might find Grant Delpit.

He could blitz off the right side. He may come in late from the left.

He might be lined up tight inside the box. He could drop deep to help in coverage.

No matter where LSU's star safety is positioned, you'd better keep your eye on him. If you're a fan, you could miss a big play. And if you're an opponent, you could be in trouble.

LSU defensive coordinator Dave Aranda had Delpit switch positions early in the year to compensate for an injured teammate. Later in the season, he was the injured player and the Tigers' defense suffered from Delpit being limited by a sore ankle.

That didn't stop Delpit from winning the Thorpe Award as the nation's top defensive back or keep No. 1 LSU (14-0) from reaching the College Football Playoff with a perfect record.

In a case of fortuitous timing for the Tigers, Delpit heads into the national championship game against No. 3 Clemson (14-0) on Jan. 13 in New Orleans feeling healthy and playing about as well as he has all season. No coincidence, the same goes for LSU's defense across the board.

"You know, I give a lot of credit to Grant and Bill Busch and Corey Raymond," Coach Aranda said. "I think they have done a great job in the back end. I remember in the summer time studying the Pittsburgh Steelers. And I had our video guy (Doug Aucoin), he gave us the last two years of Troy Polamalu on the Pittsburgh Steelers defense.

"I'm on family vacation studying the Pittsburgh Steelers and how they used Troy Polamalu, and they moved him all over and rushed him off the edge and he was such a force. So really, I had that in mind for Grant seeing his ability to rush and cover and set edges in the run game.

"Grant was open to it. We talked about it in summer time and spring ball. It wasn't really an issue or a concern. And once we got to summer, it was something he wanted to do, and it was full-go in fall camp, and I think he has really excelled in that role."

Delpit's season took a turn after teammate Todd Harris was lost for the year with a right knee injury in the third game of the season against Northwestern State.

Harris had played free safety and Delpit was slotted as a strong safety. From that spot, the 6-foot-3, 205-pound junior wreaked havoc on offenses last year and stuffed the stat sheet. He had five interceptions, five sacks, 9.5 tackles for loss and 14 passes defended to become an AP All-American in 2018. He established himself as a possible future first-round pick in the NFL draft.

Without Harris, Delpit moved into the vacated role because he was best suited to be LSU's last line of defense. That put Delpit farther from the line of scrimmage, with fewer opportunities to blitz and run to the ball.

JaCoby Stevens has played Delpit's role this season. The junior has three interceptions, is second on the team in tackles with 85 and has five sacks among 8.5 tackles for loss.

"I'm all about the results of the team," Delpit said. "So whatever position they put me at, I'm going to play it. I was playing a lot of free safety this year in the middle of the field, and just trying to get other guys in position to make plays like JaCoby being down around the ball a lot."

"Grant's a great, great player. Great young man, very unselfish. He'll do whatever it takes for the team to be successful."
-LSU head coach Ed Orgeron

Delpit's season took another turn in late October when he sprained his ankle against Auburn.

He played through the injury in the Tigers' No. 1 vs. No. 2 showdown against Alabama, a game in which the Crimson Tide passed for 419 yards, and the next week when Mississippi ran for 402 yards.

Delpit took a week off against Arkansas. When he returned, the Tigers played two of their best defensive games of the season, against Texas A&M and then Georgia in the Southeastern Conference championship game.

"Yeah, the ankle was hurting pretty bad the second half of the season a little bit, but now towards the end of it it's feeling pretty good," Delpit said. "I consider myself close to 100%, so it shouldn't be a problem."

"He was being tough all year and battling through injuries, and he got healthy towards the end of the year, and that was kind of the turning point of our defense," LSU quarterback Joe Burrow said. "I think that just shows how important he is."

"Grant's a great, great player," LSU head coach Ed Orgeron said. "Great young man, very unselfish. Look if we put him back in the post all day he's going to say, 'Coach, I'll play in the post, whatever it takes for the team.'"

Delpit was one of several important defensive players for LSU who were in and out of the lineup this season.

An ankle injury also slowed top-pass rusher K'Lavon Chaisson. The sophomore has been a terror lately and had two sacks in the semifinal victory against Oklahoma. Linebacker Michael Divinity, who sat out the last six games for what the school called personal reasons, is expected to play in the championship game.

Trevor Lawrence and Clemson will face maybe the best version of the LSU defense the Tigers have fielded all season.

"I think after the Ole Miss game, it was kind of a turnaround for us," Delpit said. "It wasn't our best performance, and I think we sat down as a defense and just saw what we did wrong, understood that some teams might try to make those plays and run it against us again. And I think we just kind of lit a fire and started playing LSU football after that. So hopefully this last game we can keep it going." ■

# LSU 36, MISSISSIPPI STATE 13
## OCTOBER 19, 2019 | STARKVILLE, MISSISSIPPI

# Defense Leads Way
## Joe Burrow throws 4 TDs passes, No. 2 LSU routs MSU

Joe Burrow didn't necessarily show his best side Saturday. While being dragged to the ground by his pants during his third sack of the game, the LSU quarterback's rear end was briefly exposed.

"I heard there was supposed to be a full moon in Starkville tonight," Burrow joked.

The rest of his performance was anything but obscene. Burrow threw for 327 yards and four touchdowns to break the LSU season record with 29 in the No. 2 Tigers' 36-13 victory over Mississippi State.

"It's a testament to him, the receivers, the offensive line, the coaches," LSU coach Ed Orgeron said. "But we're just getting started. Our team is not satisfied."

In his postgame comments, Burrows placed himself squarely in that category.

"If we play like this next week (versus No. 11 Auburn), we'll lose," Burrow said. "I think we're going to have to execute much better in the red zone than we did this week, because I don't think we'll get as many chances."

On paper, it's hard to find fault in the final results. LSU (7-0, 3-0 Southeastern Conference) had 415 yards of total offense and averaged 6.9 yards per play. The Tigers forced three turnovers, including a momentum-shifting interception right before half.

But Mississippi State (3-4, 1-3) regularly confounded the Tigers on third down. LSU struggled to find its rhythm on offense in the first half and was forced to settle for field goals on its first three drives.

"We didn't play our best game today, but I knew this day was going to come, and I'm proud of our defense," Orgeron said. "The defense came to play today. Your offense is not going to play great, on fire every week."

The safety due of JaCoby Stevens and Grant Delpit led the defensive effort.

Delpit spent the day racing downhill with his ears pinned back, racking up a team-high 11 tackles, while Stevens popped up everywhere, with a sack, an interception, and a tackle for loss to go along with eight tackles.

Delpit credited defensive coordinator Dave Aranda for opening up his arsenal to the LSU defense. Last year, it was Aranda's creation of the quarter position that spurred Delpit into All-American success. Saturday, likewise, it was Delpit's move back toward the line of scrimmage at Aranda's insistence that spurred an All-American performance.

Mississippi State quarterback Garrett Shrader (6) is drilled by Tigers safety JaCoby Stevens (3) during the second half.
WESLEY HITT / GETTY IMAGES

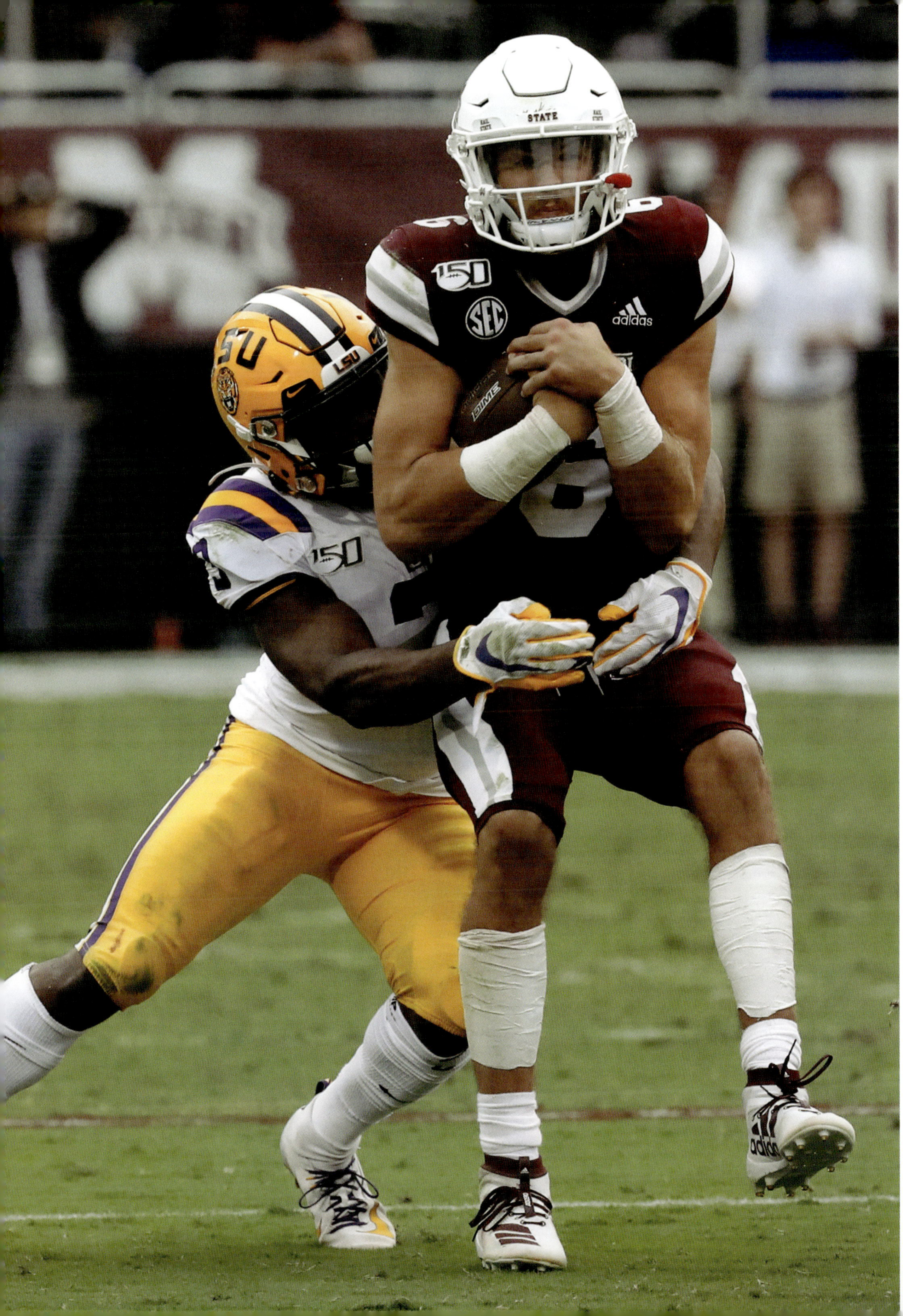
STATE
150
SEC
adidas
LSU
150
adidas

Tigers safety JaCoby Stevens (3) heads upfield with an interception of a pass intended for Mississippi State wide receiver Stephen Guidry (1) during the first action. ROGELIO V. SOLIS / AP PHOTO

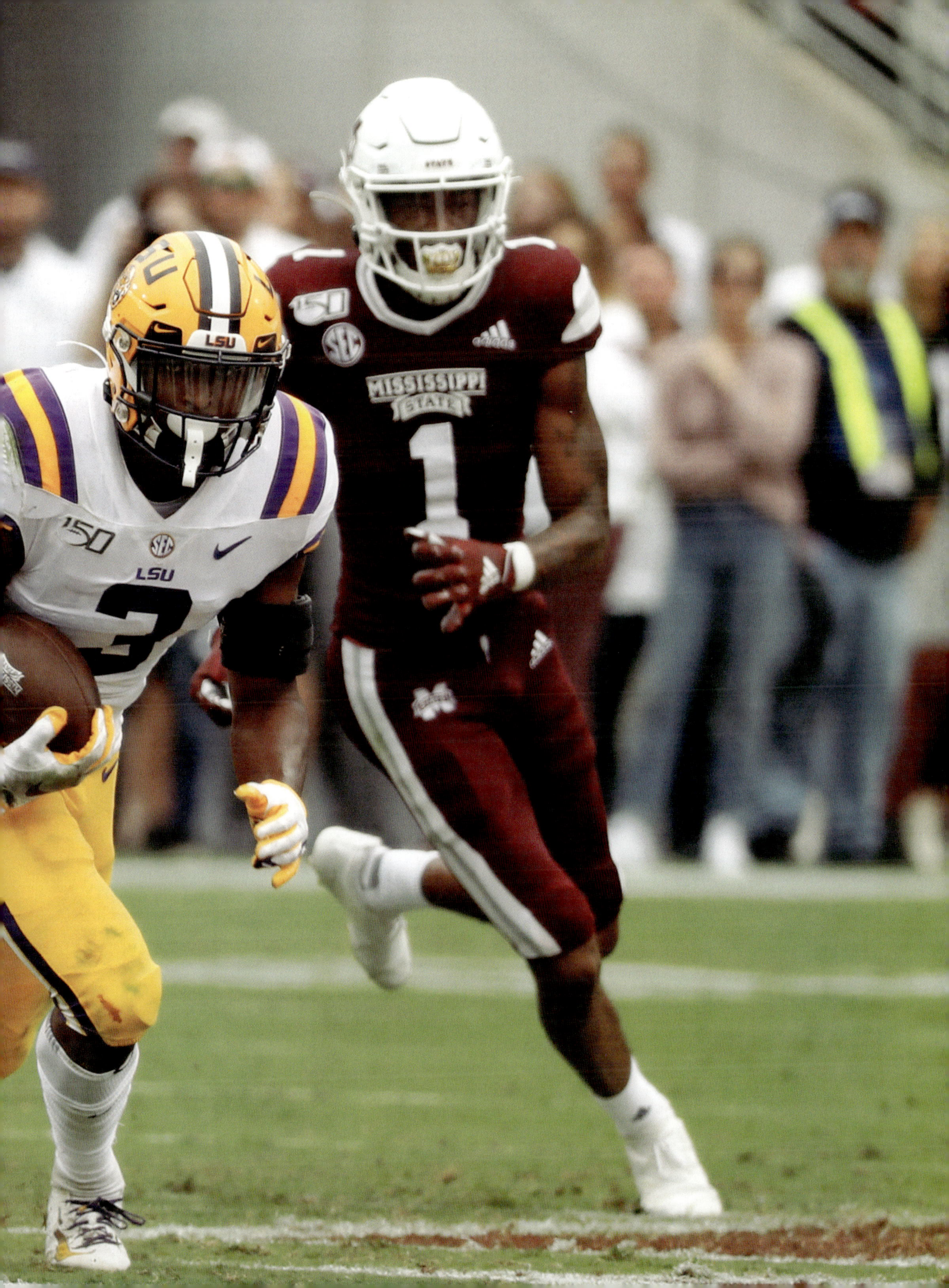
LSU
150
SEC
MISSISSIPPI
STATE
1
3

"Coach Aranda's opened it up a little bit," Delpit said. "I love when he opens it up. That's when the genius comes out."

"In my head, we were always the best safety duo in the country," said Stevens. "Today, we finally put a good game together."

The Tigers managed to score points on every drive of the first half and led 22-7 at the break. A pair of third-quarter touchdowns sealed the win.

"We just started off slow," Burrows said. "We didn't execute, and I didn't feel as much energy before the game. Early this morning you could tell that people weren't quite as locked in as they had been. But it's still good to get an SEC win."

Burrows was 25 of 32 and again threw prolifically to Justin Jefferson and Ja'Marr Chase. Jefferson had eight catches for 89 yards and a touchdown. Chase had five catches for 48 yards and a touchdown. Racey McMath and Derrick Dillon also caught TD passes.

"It just shows the amount of work we put in over the off season," Burrows said.

Mississippi State freshman Garrett Shrader threw for 238 yards and a touchdown with two interceptions. He also rushed for 66 yards and another touchdown. Kylin Hill, the SEC's No. 2 rusher, had only 34 yards and was held below 100 yards for the third straight game. Mississippi State had 13 penalties for 109 yards.

"When the margin for error is invisible, you can't turn the ball over three times against a team this good and expect to win," Bulldogs coach Joe Moorhead said. "And certainly those 13 penalties, some of that pre-snap stuff, it may not be on the front of it, but it's going to help get you beat against a team like this." ∎

**ABOVE:** Tigers linebacker Damone Clark (35) gets help from his teammates to tackle Mississippi State quarterback Garrett Shrader (6) for a loss. ROGELIO V. SOLIS / AP PHOTO

**OPPOSITE:** Tigers wide receiver Justin Jefferson, left, fights off a tackle by Mississippi State cornerback Jarrian Jones to pick up extra yards after a short pass reception. WESLEY HITT / GETTY IMAGES

# LSU 23, AUBURN 20

OCTOBER 26, 2019 | BATON ROUGE, LOUISIANA

# True Grit

## Burrow's 321 yards helps No. 2 LSU down No. 9 Auburn

Joe Burrow bounced up immediately from a high-speed hit that looked like it could have given the LSU quarterback whiplash as he was sent crashing into the Auburn bench area.

Trotting resolutely back to the line of scrimmage, Burrow resumed his school-record eighth career 300-yard passing performance in a tense, top-10 clash that put a premium on grit and perseverance.

Burrow passed for 321 yards and a touchdown, ran for 47 yards and another score, and second-ranked LSU edged No. 9 Auburn 23-20 on Saturday.

"If your quarterback shows toughness like that, it can kind of get your team going," Burrow said. "If you lay down on the field and don't hop right back up, it shows your team that you are not really into it."

The victory ensured LSU (8-0, 4-0 SEC) would be unbeaten heading into its highly anticipated Nov. 9 tilt at Alabama, which entered this weekend ranked No. 1.

Clyde Edwards-Helaire rushed for 136 yards and touchdown for LSU, which wasn't able to put away Auburn (6-2, 3-2) until Derrick Dillon recovered an onside kick with 2:31 left.

"It was a gut check tonight," LSU coach Ed Orgeron said, praising the way his players stuck together. "They didn't want to be denied."

While LSU's prolific, up-tempo spread offense rolled up 508 yards, the unit didn't approach its 50.1-point scoring average against an Auburn defense that thwarted LSU drives into its territory with a pair of fourth-down stops and an interception.

"They fought their guts out and our defense played unbelievable," Auburn coach Gus Malzahn said. "We had opportunities and we didn't seize the moment. We just didn't get it done offensively."

LSU had not previously scored fewer than 36 points in a game, but Auburn's defensive front put pressure on Burrow, sacking him three times.

Still, Burrow didn't flinch when he was leveled along the sideline after 14-yard scramble on third-and-12 in the first half. He completed five of his next six throws, ending with a 20-yard touchdown on a fade to Terrace Marshall Jr.

Burrow completed 32 of 42 passes. His top target was Ja'Marr Chase, who caught eight passes for 123 yards.

"We showed toughness today. It was not a pretty win by any means," Burrow said. "SEC games aren't going to be pretty. When you can come out on top of a top-10 team and feel like you could have played better, it's always a good thing."

Tigers quarterback Joe Burrow (9) celebrates with Clyde Edwards-Helaire (22) after rushing for a touchdown.
JOHN KORDUNER / ICON SPORTSWIRE VIA GETTY IMAGES

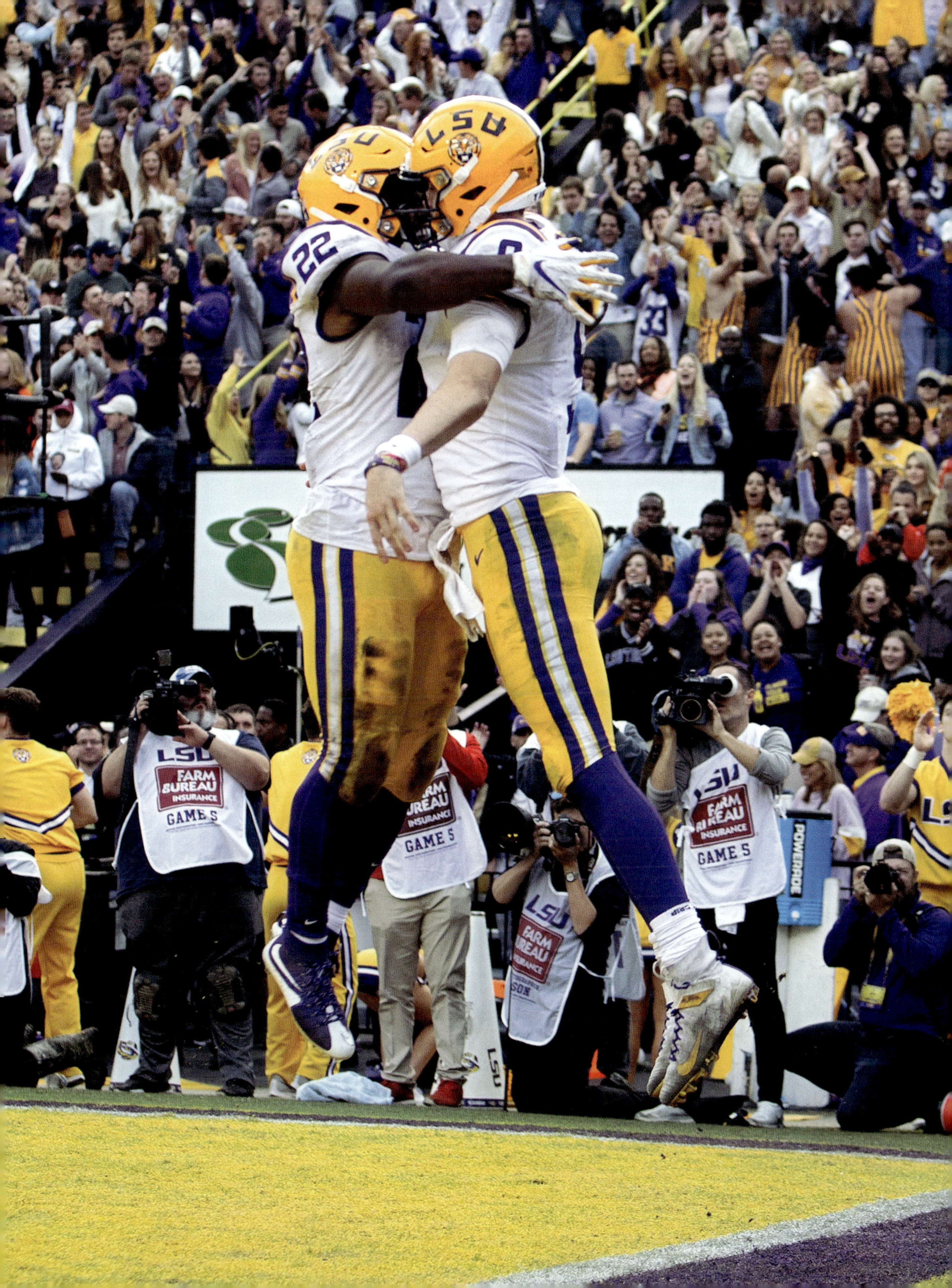
LSU
22
FARM BUREAU INSURANCE
GAME 5
POWERADE

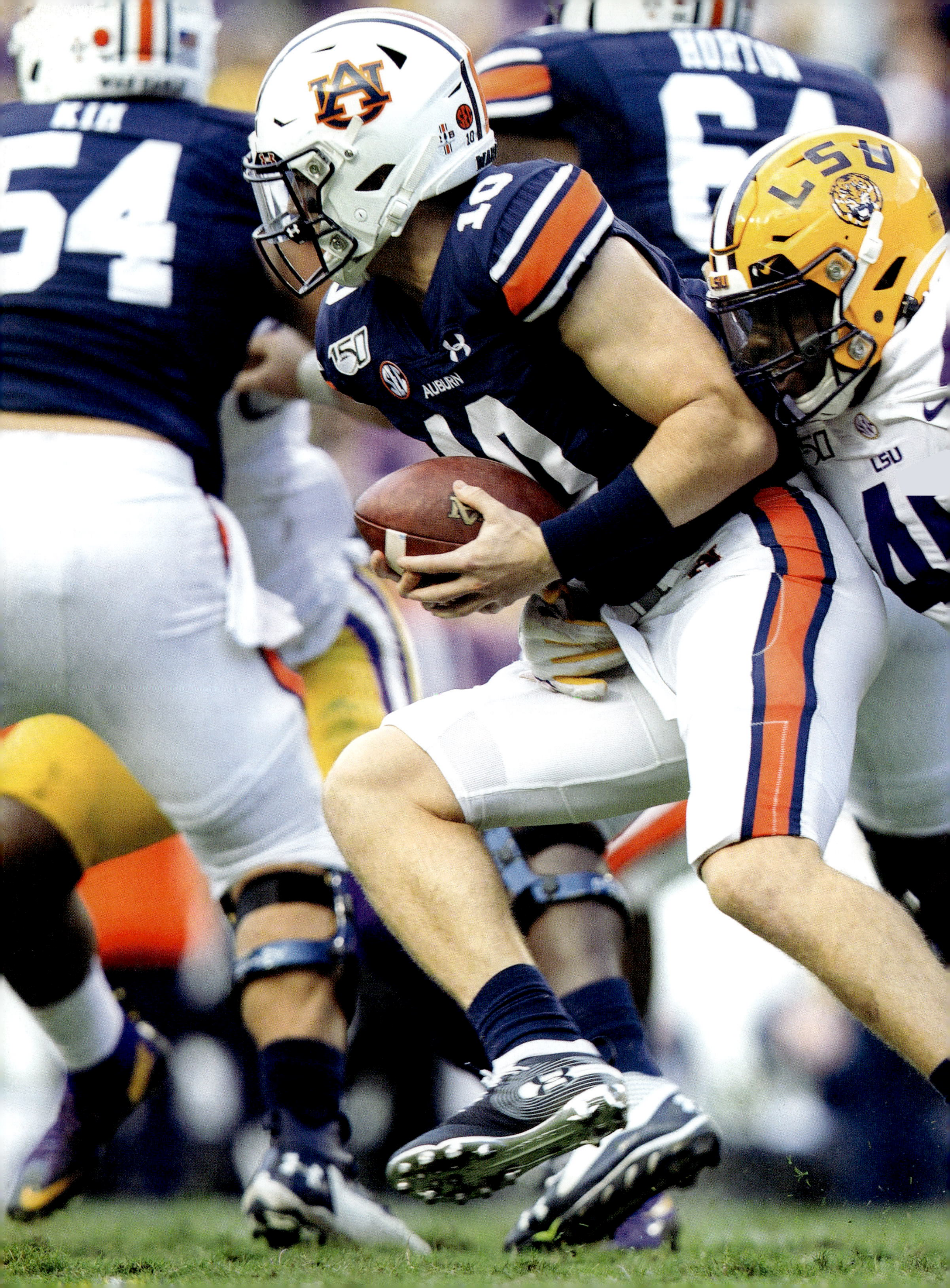
KIM
54
HORTON
10
AUBURN
LSU

Tigers linebacker Michael Divinity Jr. (45) sacks Auburn Tigers quarterback Bo Nix (10).
CHRIS GRAYTHEN / GETTY IMAGES

**ABOVE:** Quarterback Joe Burrow (9) scampers up field on a second half carry. CHRIS GRAYTHEN / GETTY IMAGES

**OPPOSITE:** Tigers cornerback Derek Stingley Jr. (24) and safety JaCoby Stevens (3) break up a pass intended for Auburn wide receiver Seth Williams (18). GERALD HERBERT / AP PHOTO

Bo Nix completed 15 of 35 passes for 157 yards and one late touchdown to Seth Williams that gave Auburn the opportunity to set up a meaningful onside kick.

D.J. Williams rushed for 130 yards for Auburn, which looked primed to go ahead by a touchdown in the third quarter when Williams sprinted into the open field from his own 20.

Safety Grant Delpit forced Williams out of bounds just inside the 10, and Auburn couldn't parlay the 70-yard run into a touchdown, settling for a field goal to make it 13-10.

That lead lasted until five minutes remained in the third quarter, in part because Burrow's screen to Chase was stopped on fourth-and-goal from the Auburn 2. Later in the quarter, Burrow's pass intended for Chase was intercepted by Roger McCreary at the Auburn 2.

LSU hadn't trailed that late in a game all season, but LSU finally pushed in front by going back to a running game that had struggled most of the first three quarters. Edwards-Helaire ran four straight times for gains for 45 yards, capped by his 6-yard score to put LSU in front 16-13.

Burrow's 7-yard rushing TD, capping another run-heavy drive, widened the lead to 23-13.

"I think a lesser team would not have won that game tonight," Orgeron said. "They got up ahead, but our guys kept on fighting." ∎

# LSU 46, ALABAMA 41

NOVEMBER 9, 2019 | TUSCALOOSA, ALABAMA

# Drought Over

## After eight years LSU finally beats Alabama

Joe Burrow passed for 393 yards and three touchdowns and No. 2 LSU (No. 1 in AP) snapped an eight-game losing streak to No. 3 Alabama (No. 2 in AP) with a 46-41 victory Saturday.

The Tigers (9-0, 5-0 Southeastern Conference) are no longer second fiddle in the SEC West, or maybe in the playoff rankings. And Burrow stamped himself as the Heisman Trophy front-runner with a gutty performance when he answered every challenge from Bama.

And the challenges were plentiful.

The Crimson Tide (8-1, 5-1) rallied from a 33-13 halftime deficit to three times pull within a touchdown in the fourth quarter. It kept going from game seemingly over to game on.

The showdown lived up to its billing as a duel between two high-powered offenses and star quarterbacks with President Donald Trump attending. Tua Tagovailoa launched an 85-yard touchdown pass to DeVonta Smith with 1:21 left after the Tigers' own scoring march.

Justin Jefferson recovered the onside kick, and LSU ran out the clock.

Burrow completed 31 of 39 passes and ran for 64 yards and was carried most of the way off the field by two teammates.

That's what Burrow sought when he transferred to LSU from Ohio State.

"That was pretty special, you know," Burrow said. "Having the guys embrace me the way they have, just some quarterback from Ohio who came in last June before the season, it means a lot to me. And we're not done yet. It's Game 9. We've got three more regular-season ones and the SEC championship. We've got bigger goals than this."

"He's one of the best we've had here," LSU coach Ed Orgeron said of his two-year starting quarterback. "But we've still got four games left and we're going down the road, we're going to try to win every game and we're going to bring a championship back to Louisiana."

Clyde Edwards-Helaire, the Tigers' 5-foot-8 locomotive engine, was a mostly overlooked three-star prospect who starred at Baton Rouge's Catholic High School and decided to stay home to play college football. On Saturday he rushed for 103 yards and three touchdowns in 20 carries and caught nine passes for 77 yards and a touchdown, getting emotional on the sideline after a late touchdown that appeared once again to put the game away.

"He's an outstanding man from Louisiana," Orgeron said. "I'm proud of him."

Quarterback Joe Burrow (9) is carried off the field by teammates Tyler Shelvin (72) and Zach Von Rosenberg (38) after defeating Alabama.
KEVIN C. COX / GETTY IMAGES

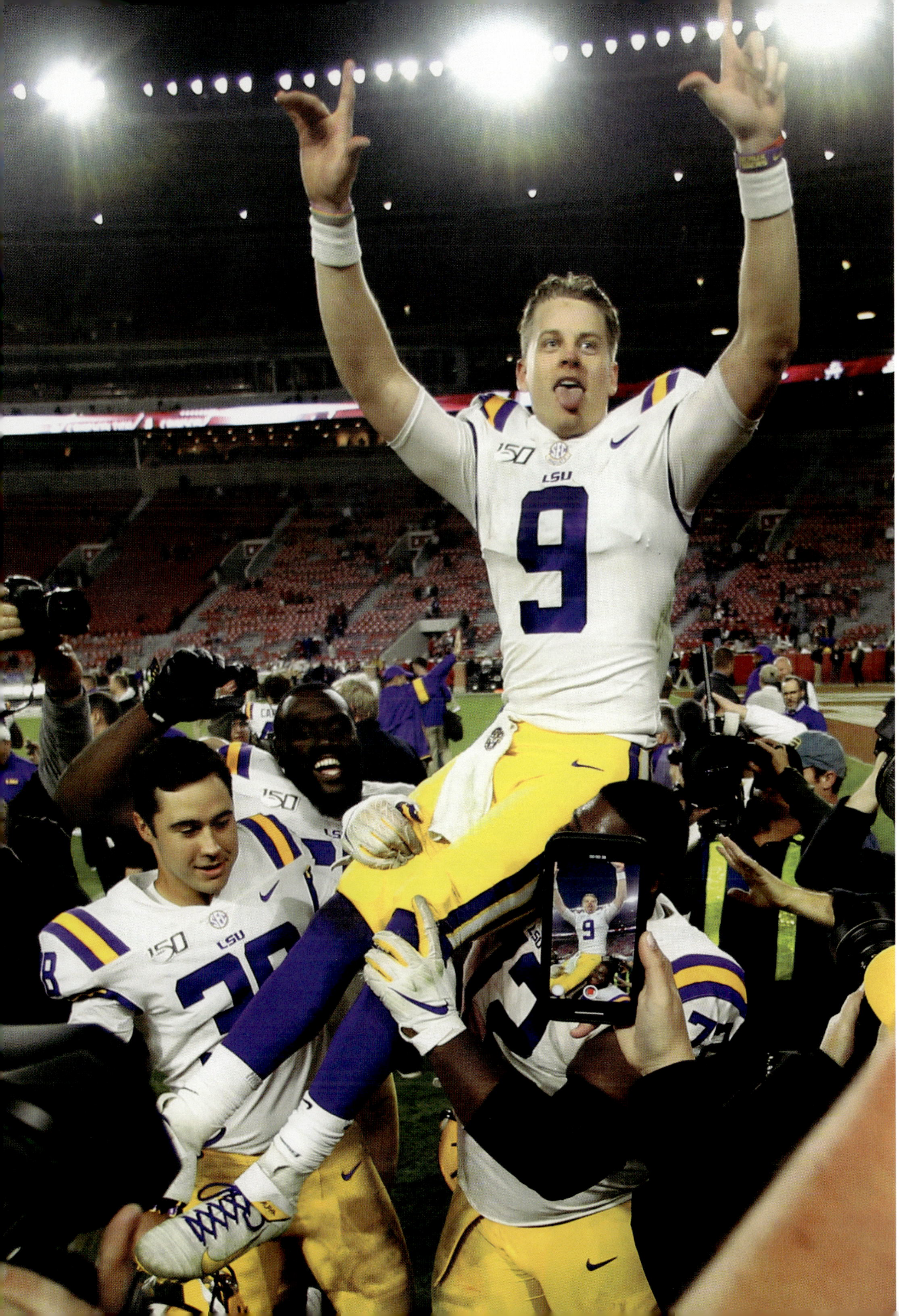
LSU
9

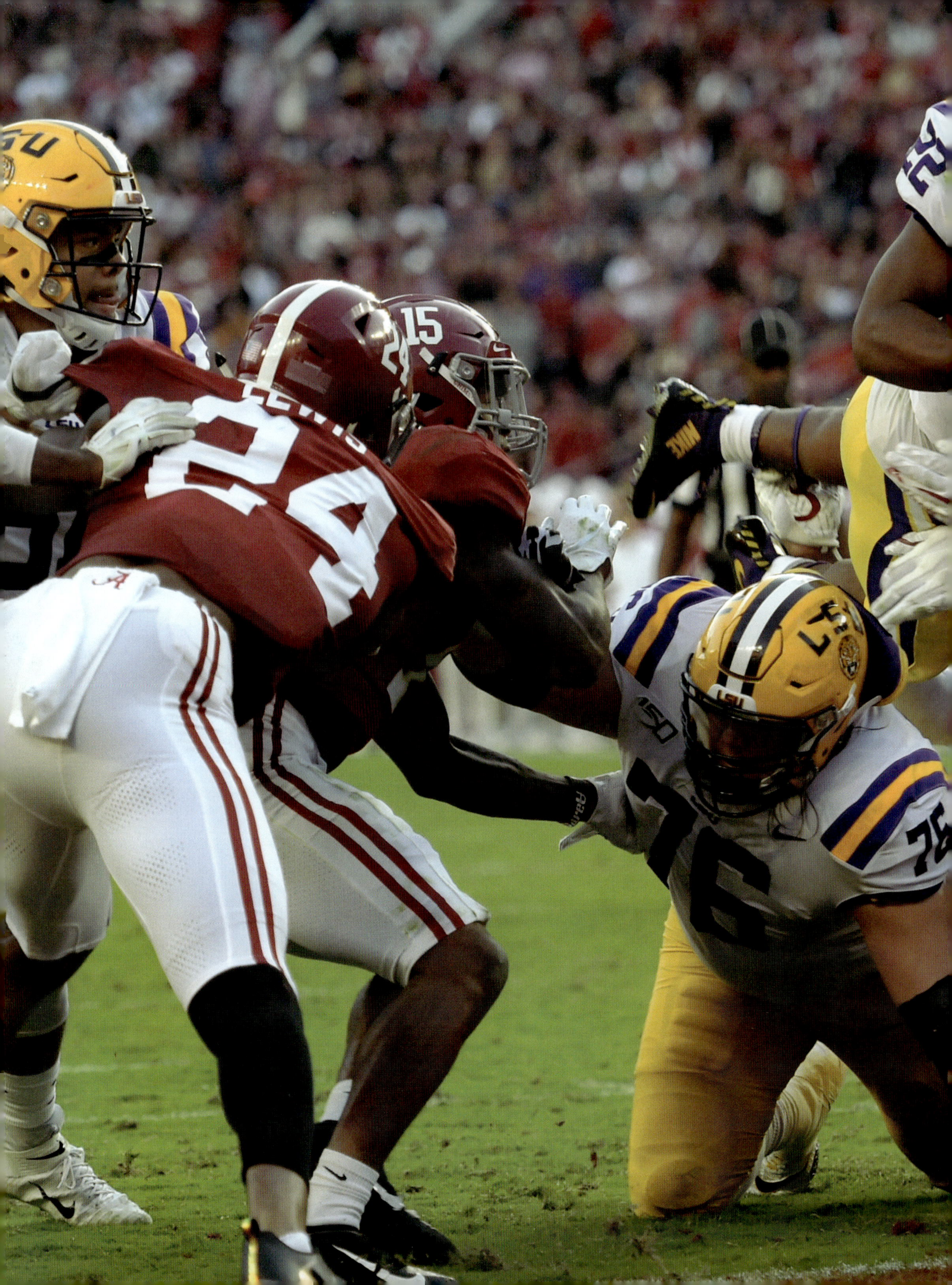
15
24
76
NIKE

LSU running back Clyde Edwards-Helaire (22) dives over Alabama's Raekwon Davis (99) and Markail Benton (36) for a second quarter touchdown. KEVIN C. COX / GETTY IMAGES

Tigers safety JaCoby Stevens (3) recovers Alabama quarterback Tua Tagovailoa's (13) first quarter fumble.
KEVIN C. COX / GETTY IMAGES

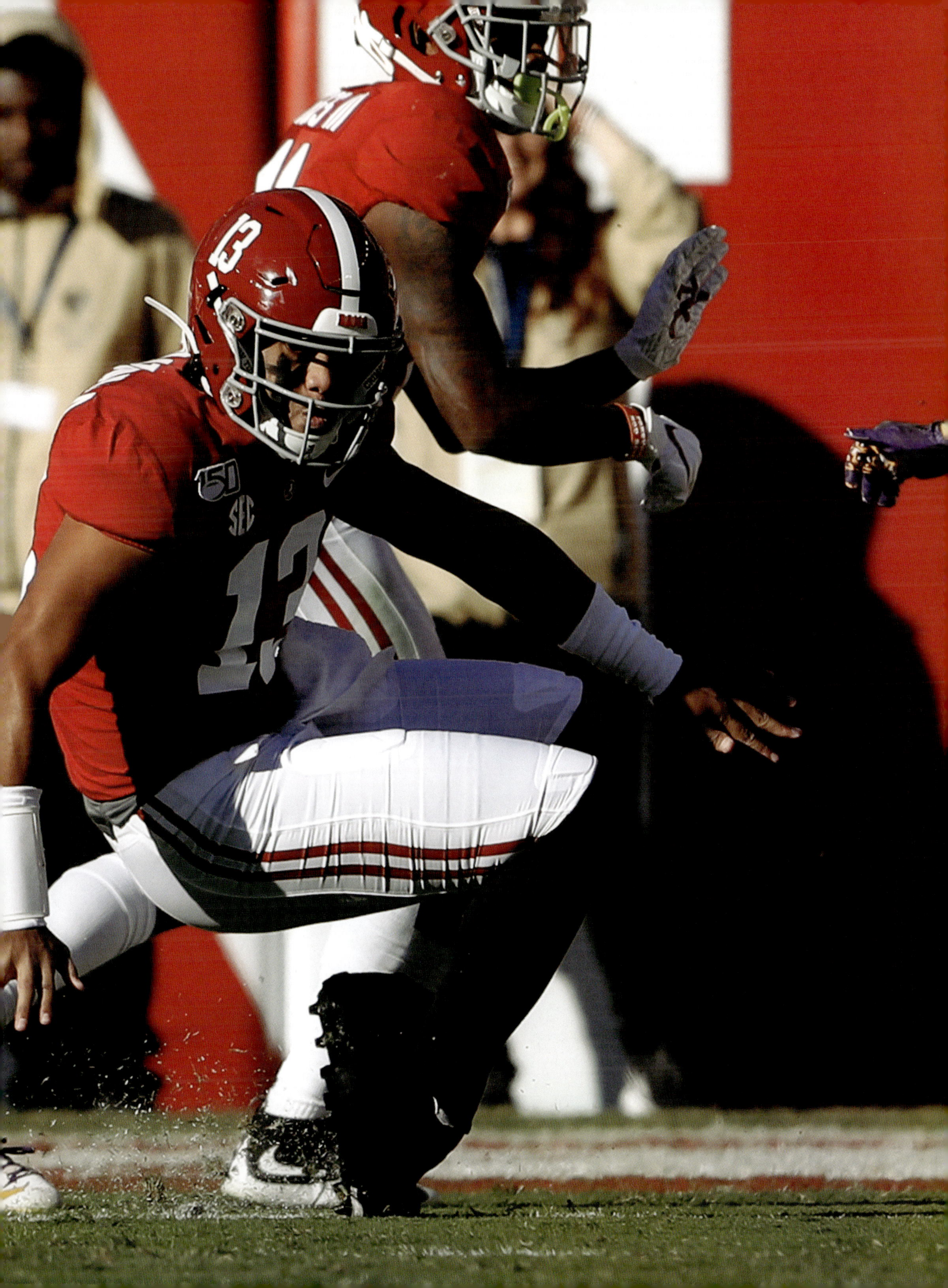
13
150
SEC
13

**ABOVE:** Tigers wide receiver Ja'Marr Chase (1) goes up high for the touchdown catch as Alabama defensive back Trevon Diggs (7) defends. JOHN BAZEMORE / AP PHOTO

**OPPOSITE:** LSU head coach Ed Orgeron embraces quarterback Joe Burrow (9) after defeating Alabama 46-41. KEVIN C. COX / GETTY IMAGES

Tagovailoa, 20 days removed from ankle surgery, was 21-of-40 for 418 yards and four touchdowns with an interception and a fumble. He was called a "game-time decision" all week, looked shaky early and appeared to be limping after the game, but he kept Alabama in it.

Coach Nick Saban said Tagovailoa practiced all week without any issues.

"He said he could play in the game, he wanted to play in the game and he thought he could go out and do a good job," Saban said. "I think he was a warrior in terms of what he did."

LSU outgained Alabama by a slender 559-541. The Tigers had scored just 39 combined points in the previous five meetings.

"I told them on Monday, we're the better football team," Orgeron said. "That's the first time I've told this team that going into Alabama. When I got on the plane coming here, I felt like, 'You know what, we got 'em. We finally got the tools we need, we finally got the players we need, we finally got the coaching staff we need to beat these guys."

Make no mistake, this win was for Louisiana.

For eight years of losing to the Crimson Tide.

"I might be able to go to the 7-Eleven now and get a Monster or a Red Bull, and they won't have to tell me, 'Coach O, you gotta beat those guys,'" Orgeron said.

"This won't be the last. We comin'. We comin'. We're going to continue to rise. We're going to continue to make progress in this program to bring a championship back to Louisiana. This is not the last time we're going to beat them. I promise you that." ∎

# The Perfect Fit

## LSU hits home-run with Orgeron hire

Ed Orgeron can't get enough of the view. He leads a visitor through a "war room" where he and a few staff members are watching film of an offensive line drill from practice, shuffles through his office and opens the double doors onto a balcony fit for a head of state.

Orgeron takes a seat and looks directly east toward Tiger Stadium towering in the distance. The old cement structure known for withstanding the kind of rousing support that results in seismic activity on fall Saturday nights sits in silence, and a full moon hangs high above, illuminating faint white clouds against a dark blue sky.

"You *kiddin'* me?" Orgeron says. "How about this place, huh?"

It is home, and yet he has never seen it quite like this. Two days have passed since Louisiana State beat Alabama in college football's latest "Game of the Century," a win that felt more like a statewide exorcism. Just like that, gone were the eight long years of Nick Saban's tyranny, and gone were the fears that one of their own would never rise up and take down the one who got away.

The party started as soon as running back Clyde Edwards-Helaire iced the game with a late seven-yard touchdown run Saturday and raged through the holiday weekend. It is finally dying down now on this peaceful Monday night, as the faithful prepare to return to their lives.

But how could there ever be normalcy again? The 9-0 Tigers are No. 1 in every poll in the land. This should be Orgeron's moment, but the native son of Lafourche Parish doesn't claim it as his own.

"I felt it," Orgeron says in his trademark rumbling growl. "I felt it as a resident, as a fan, and I feel it as a coach. Freedom, man. We don't have to hear that stuff no more. I'm just happy for the people of Louisiana."

Orgeron's lofty perch from the balcony of the newly opened LSU Football Operations Center creates the impression of a king surveying his kingdom, only he wants to share the riches with everyone.

He can't take these gifts for granted, because deep down he knows it so easily could have been someone else manning the throne. Someone younger, flashier, more sellable, someone who could pass through the same central casting requirements for a big-time college football coach that Orgeron could not meet six years ago right down the road from Hollywood at USC.

If there was ever a top program that would accept the red-faced 58-year-old Cajun with the gravelly accent as a proper cultural fit, it is this one, nestled between mossy University Lake and the banks of the Mighty Mississippi. And yet, even here, he was not wanted in the role after putting together a 6-2 record as the interim head coach, just as he had done at USC before Steve Sarkisian was offered the job.

At LSU, the hot name was Tom Herman, then the coach at Houston. Since those uncertain days, Orgeron has won more games against top-10 opponents than any other coach — including one against Herman's Texas team Sept. 7 in Austin — but reliving the last week of the 2016 season still induces a tinge of terror in Orgeron's darting brown eyes.

LSU played at Texas A&M on Thanksgiving Day that year. The night before, Orgeron's

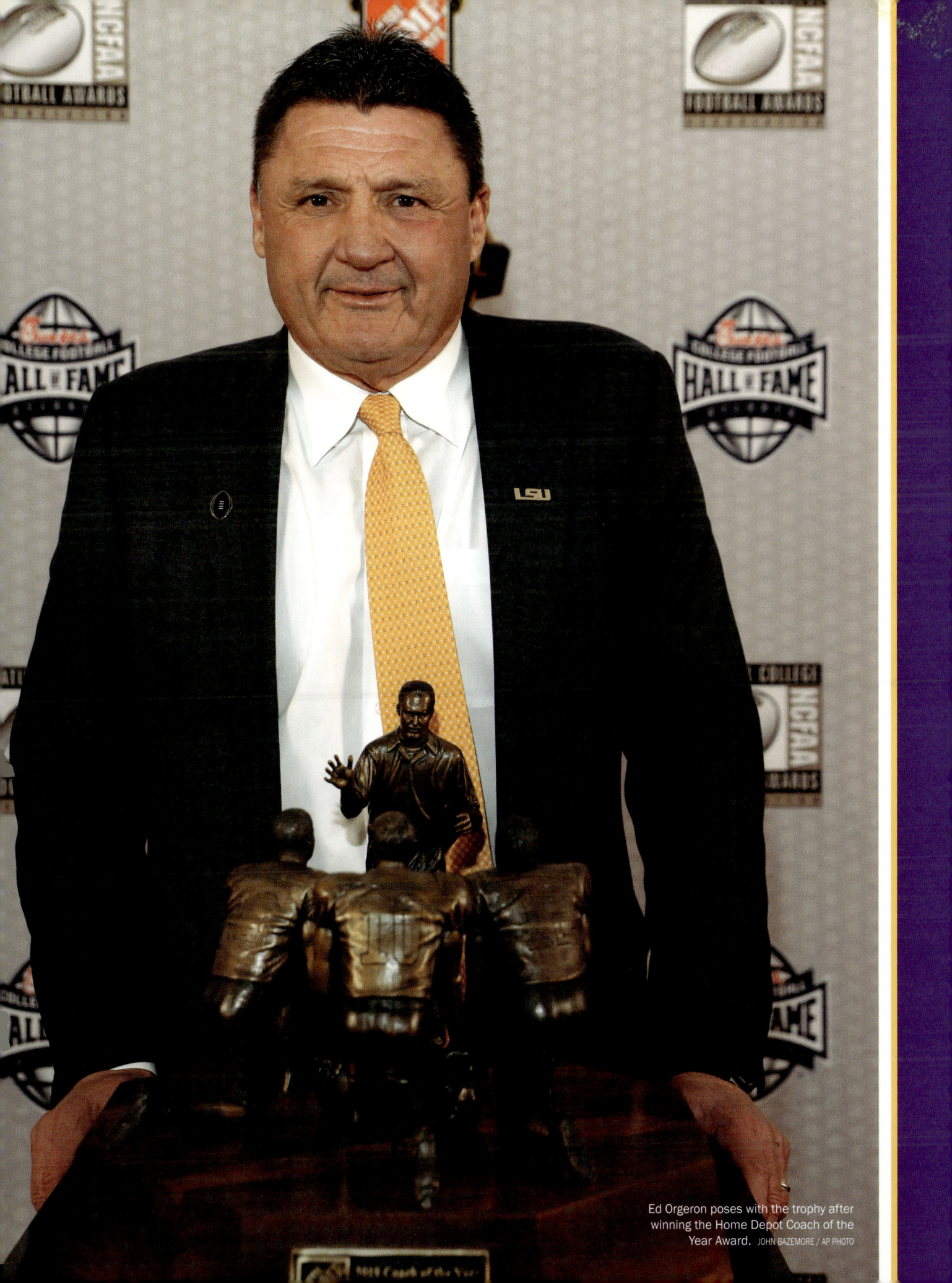

Ed Orgeron poses with the trophy after winning the Home Depot Coach of the Year Award. JOHN BAZEMORE / AP PHOTO

wife, Kelly, came back from dinner and told him that she heard LSU had offered the job to Jimbo Fisher, then the coach of Florida State. The Tigers roughed up the Aggies, but later on Thanksgiving night, a staff member told Orgeron that a report was saying LSU had offered the job to Herman.

"I said, 'That's good! Last night it was Jimbo, tonight it's Tom, maybe tomorrow it's us!'" Orgeron recalls.

He laughs at the remembrance, but it was hard to keep perspective then.

"Because I been here before, you know," Orgeron says, a subdued reference to his USC heartbreak.

The Friday after beating Texas A&M, he met with then-LSU athletic director Joe Alleva, ready to fight for what he believed was right. A couple of Orgeron's staff members had helped him compile books and manuals overflowing with creative ideas of how to bring the Tigers back to the level they achieved Saturday night in Tuscaloosa.

He felt he had already spurred a cultural transition from team into family, the Tigers' collective heart swelling and pulling their bodies further than they ever thought they could go.

But Alleva set the vast reading material aside and leveled with Orgeron.

"I gotta tell you, I'm going to meet with Tom Herman tonight," Alleva said.

"I told my staff to leave," Orgeron says. "I said, 'Joe,' and I touched him in his belly, 'You know in your belly I'm the right man for LSU. I look forward to being the next head coach of LSU,' and I walked out."

That night, at home in Mandeville, his family staged a belated Thanksgiving dinner. Orgeron felt so sick he couldn't eat. He went off to bed and prayed. Before he could fall asleep, news flashed across the ticker that Herman was expected to take the LSU job. Kelly assured him it couldn't be true, that he would wake up the next morning and be offered the position.

"I said, 'What you drinkin'?!'" Orgeron says, banging a table for effect.

In the middle of the night, Orgeron woke to his phone buzzing. Lane Kiffin, whom he had promised Alleva would be his offensive coordinator, said Herman was now reportedly leaning toward Texas. Around 5:30 a.m., Orgeron missed a call from Alleva. He frantically called back.

"Can you be here at 7:30?" Alleva asked.

In a flash, Orgeron was blazing his truck down Interstate 12. He put on his favorite song, Creedence Clearwater Revival's "Born on the Bayou," a low-country boy feeling a high he'd never experienced, before he realized something important: He hadn't been offered the job yet.

He arrived at the office and saw Alleva waiting for him by the Tiger statue at the entrance.

"You want the job or what?" Alleva said.

"I grabbed him and *shoooook* him, *maaan*!" Orgeron says.

"You know, when you pointed to my belly, all night long I was feeling something in my belly," Alleva told him.

"I said, 'I put that Cajun gravy on you, boy!'" Orgeron says with a hearty cackle.

Orgeron never asked what happened with Herman, whether he was offered the position or not. It didn't matter one bit then and still doesn't. Just check out the blessing's life has bestowed upon him.

He's head coach at a school, and in a state, he loves.

"The culture, the want-to, the toughness, being blue collar, being from Louisiana, being proud of it, having a Cajun accent," Orgeron says. "My grandparents spoke French. I'm proud of it. People make fun of the way I talk, I love it. I wouldn't change it for *nothin'*. This place is who I am" ■

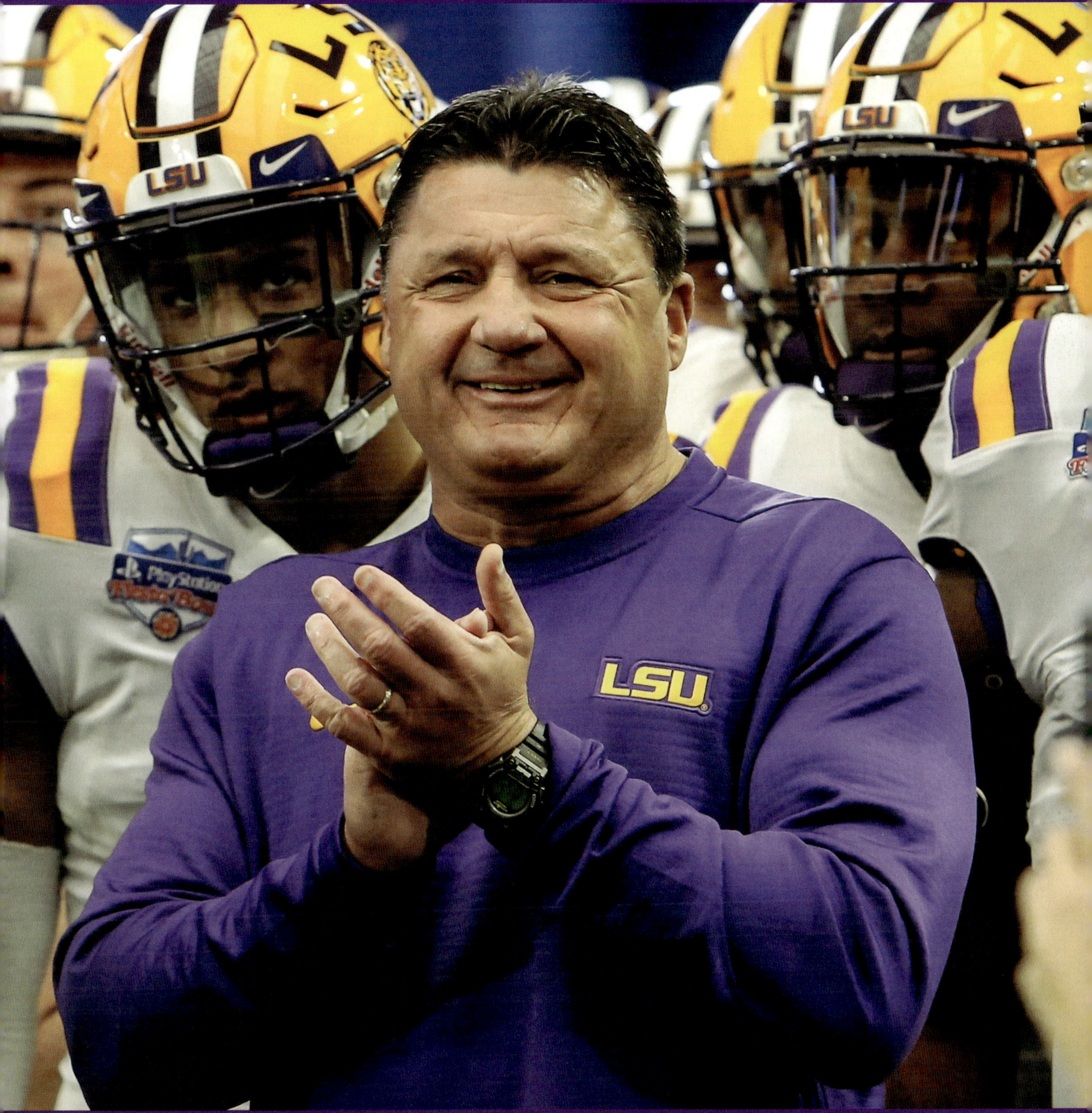
LSU

# LSU 58, MISSISSIPPI 37

NOVEMBER 16, 2019 | OXFORD, MISSISSIPPI

# A Record-Breaking Night

## Burrow sets passing record, No. 1 LSU downs Mississippi

Joe Burrow's postgame shrug pretty much summed up what kind of a season it has been for LSU.

"You know things have changed at LSU when you have 700 yards of total offense and everybody is upset in the locker room," the Heisman Trophy front-runner said.

Burrow threw for a career-best 489 yards and five touchdowns as top-ranked Tigers built a big lead and held off Mississippi 58-37 on Saturday night.

Coming off an emotional 46-41 home win at Alabama last week, the Tigers (10-0, 6-0 Southeastern Conference) scored on four of their first five possessions jump out to a 28-0 lead over the Rebels (4-7, 2-5).

The teams combined for 1,328 yards of total offense, including 714 by the Tigers. Burrow completed 32 of 42 passes, including touchdown passes of 34, 51 and 61 yards to Ja'Marr Chase (227 yards) and 12 and 7 yards to Justin Jefferson (112 yards).

No big deal. Seems Burrow is more into letters than numbers.

"Those are just numbers on a stat sheet for us," he says. "We're all about the Ws."

"Give credit to them," Burrow added. "They are a really good offense. They started to score and you can't hold down an offense like that for an entire game. We just had to keep scoring. You have to feel good about the victory though. 10-0, it can't get any better."

"It wasn't pretty, but we did it after a big win last week," LSU coach Ed Orgeron said. "We came in here to win a football game and we did that. We're 10-0 and I'm very proud of that."

Burrow completed 17 consecutive passes at one point to set a school record and passed Rohan Davey's single-season school record for yards passing set in 2001. He threw two interceptions in the second half as Ole Miss climbed closer, but put the game away with a 61-yard touchdown pass to Chase with 5:11 remaining.

"I thought he (Burrow) was on fire, especially in the first half," Orgeron said. "He made a lot of plays and extended some plays with his feet. He's a great athlete. We could probably run the zone read a little more, we just don't want to do that."

Chase and Jefferson each eclipsed 1,000 yards on the season during the contest. The duo became the third in SEC history to reach the milestone, joining LSU's Jarvis Landry and Odell Beckham Jr. in 2013, and Florida's Jabar

Tigers wide receiver Ja'Marr Chase (1) catches a 34-yard touchdown pass during the first half. JONATHAN BOCKMAN / GETTY IMAGES

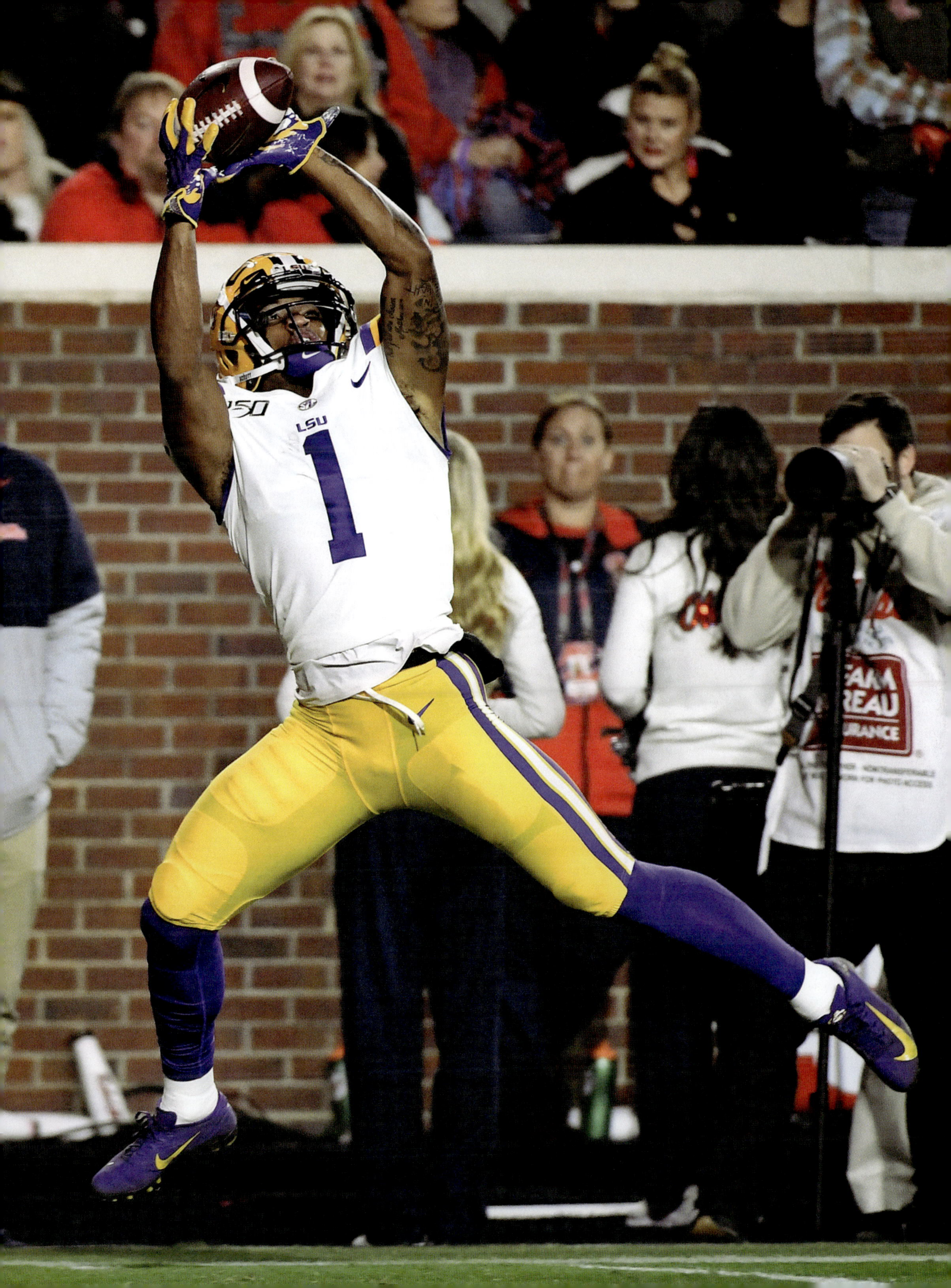
LSU
1

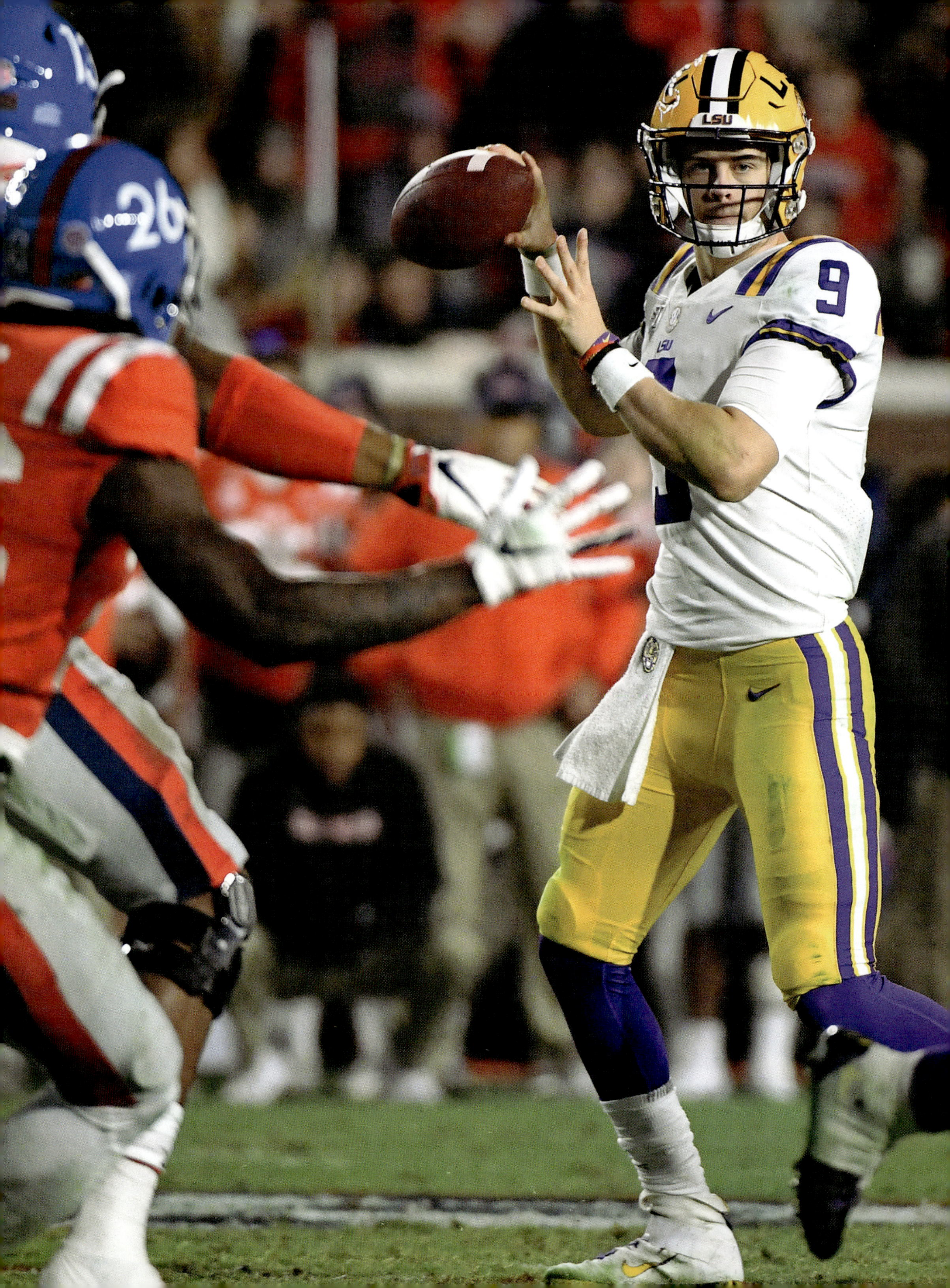
LSU
9
26

Gaffney and Reche Caldwell in 2001. Chase tied the school record with his 12th touchdown catch of the season.

The LSU signal-caller loves having two of the most dynamic receivers in the country to throw to.

"We have great timing," Burrows says of Chase and Jefferson. "They're special players who are going to play a long time. They're great people and hard workers too. That means more than anything on the football field."

Clyde Edwards-Helaire capped the scoring with a 49-yard touchdown run with 3:08 left and finished with 174 yards rushing on 23 carries.

"We dug ourselves too deep a hole," Ole Miss coach Matt Luke said. "We had a chance to get it to a one possession game, but we never could get there."

Ole Miss freshman quarterback John Rhys Plumlee had 212 yards rushing yards, a school record for a quarterbacks, and three touchdowns and was 9 of 16 passing for 123 yards.

"I need to look at it," Orgerson said about his defense. "Obviously 400 yards rushing and over 500 yards offense. You don't want that. We need to look at it. See on film where we went wrong. Schematically,

Tigers quarterback Joe Burrow (9) throws a short pass in the flat to Clyde Edwards-Helaire (22) during the second half.
THOMAS GRANING / AP PHOTO

personnel wise, technique, whatever it may be. The bottom line is when you win games, you kind of pick things apart."

"Again, our object was to win the game, and we won by 21 points," Orgeron said. "We expected a fight. The first half was easier than I thought it would be. I thought we controlled them well in the first half, and obviously in the second half they started making plays. We had to fight and the turnover hurt us. We couldn't stop Plumlee but we won the football game. (Burrow) broke a record and so did Ja'Marr. We're going to get better. I have to remind them (team) right now to enjoy the win." ■

Tigers running back Tyrion Davis-Price (3) carries the ball for a 4-yard touchdown run.
THOMAS GRANING / AP PHOTO

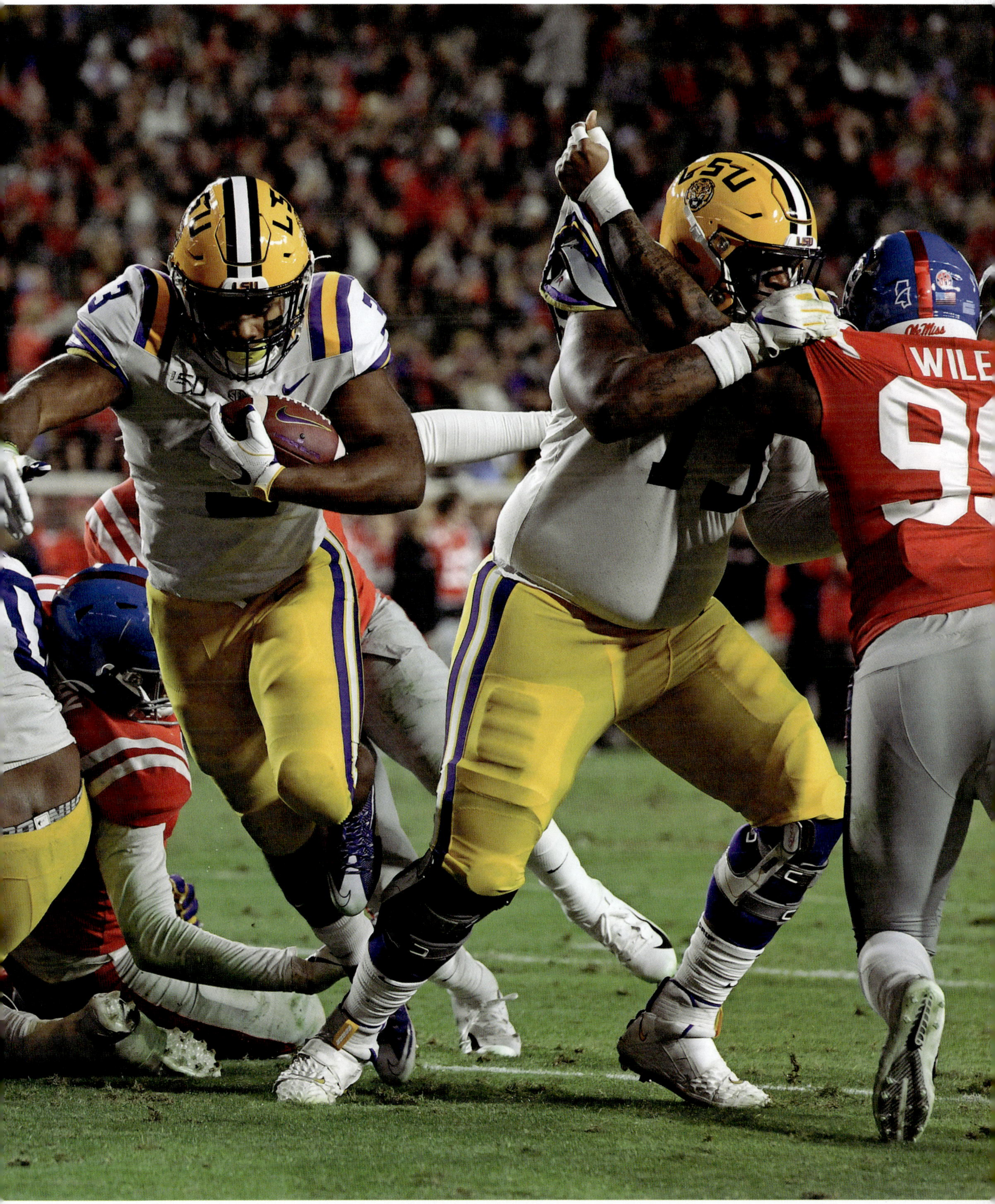
WILE

# LSU 56, ARKANSAS 20
## NOVEMBER 23, 2019 | BATON ROUGE, LOUISIANA

# Hogtied
## No. 1 LSU books SEC title game berth

LSU coaches called one last play for running back Clyde Edwards-Helaire in hopes of getting him his fourth-straight 100-yard game.

Perhaps it was only fitting that Edwards-Helaire, who needed just a yard, would break loose for a career-long 89-yard touchdown run. The top-ranked Tigers' new spread offense has been producing explosive plays all season—a big reason why they've booked a trip to the Southeastern Conference title game for the first time since 2011.

Joe Burrow passed for 327 yards and three touchdowns, Edwards-Helaire rushed for a career-high 188 yards and three TDs and No. 1 LSU remained unbeaten with a 56-20 victory over reeling Arkansas on Saturday night.

"What a showing on offense – and we're not done yet," LSU head coach Ed Orgeron said, referring as much to all 11 games this season as to the Tigers' 612 total yards against Arkansas.

While LSU won "The Boot," a gold trophy in the shape of the states of Arkansas and Louisiana, the Tigers didn't celebrate with it.

"There wasn't going to be too much of a celebration to beat Arkansas. They haven't beat anybody in a long time," Orgeron said. "We don't feel like we've accomplished what we want to accomplish yet."

LSU (11-0, 7-0) can finish no worse than in a tie for first with Alabama (10-1, 6-1) in the SEC West and owns the tiebreaker with its 46-41 triumph in Tuscaloosa on Nov. 9.

"We expected this coming into the year. If we were not 11-0 right now, we would be disappointed," Burrow said. "That's a testament to our hard work, but we've got more ahead of us."

Each time Edwards-Helaire broke loose for a score — his other TDs went for 27 and 26 yards — he left at least one defensive back grasping at air. On his 89-yarder, he was about to be caught from behind but used a high-step to slip the tackle before resuming his gallop to the goal line as the Tiger Stadium crowd roared for a Baton Rouge native having a career night.

"Everybody's talking about breakaway speed," Edwards-Helaire said, a nod to critics of his ability to finish runs in the open field. "I hope that was fast enough for everybody. I went in and it was like, `Get the yard, get out of bounds, shut it down for the rest of the game," said the diminutive back, who has 15 TDs rushing this season. "But that hole parted like the Red Sea."

"I knew Clyde was going to have a lot of success for us and I knew that this offense fit him perfectly. We use him like that guy over there in New Orleans," Burrow said, referring to Saints running back Alvin Kamara.

Burrow's first touchdown was a 37-yarder

Tigers linebacker Jacob Phillips (6) gives the one gun salute after sacking Arkansas quarterback K.J. Jefferson during the first half.
MATTHEW HINTON / AP PHOTO

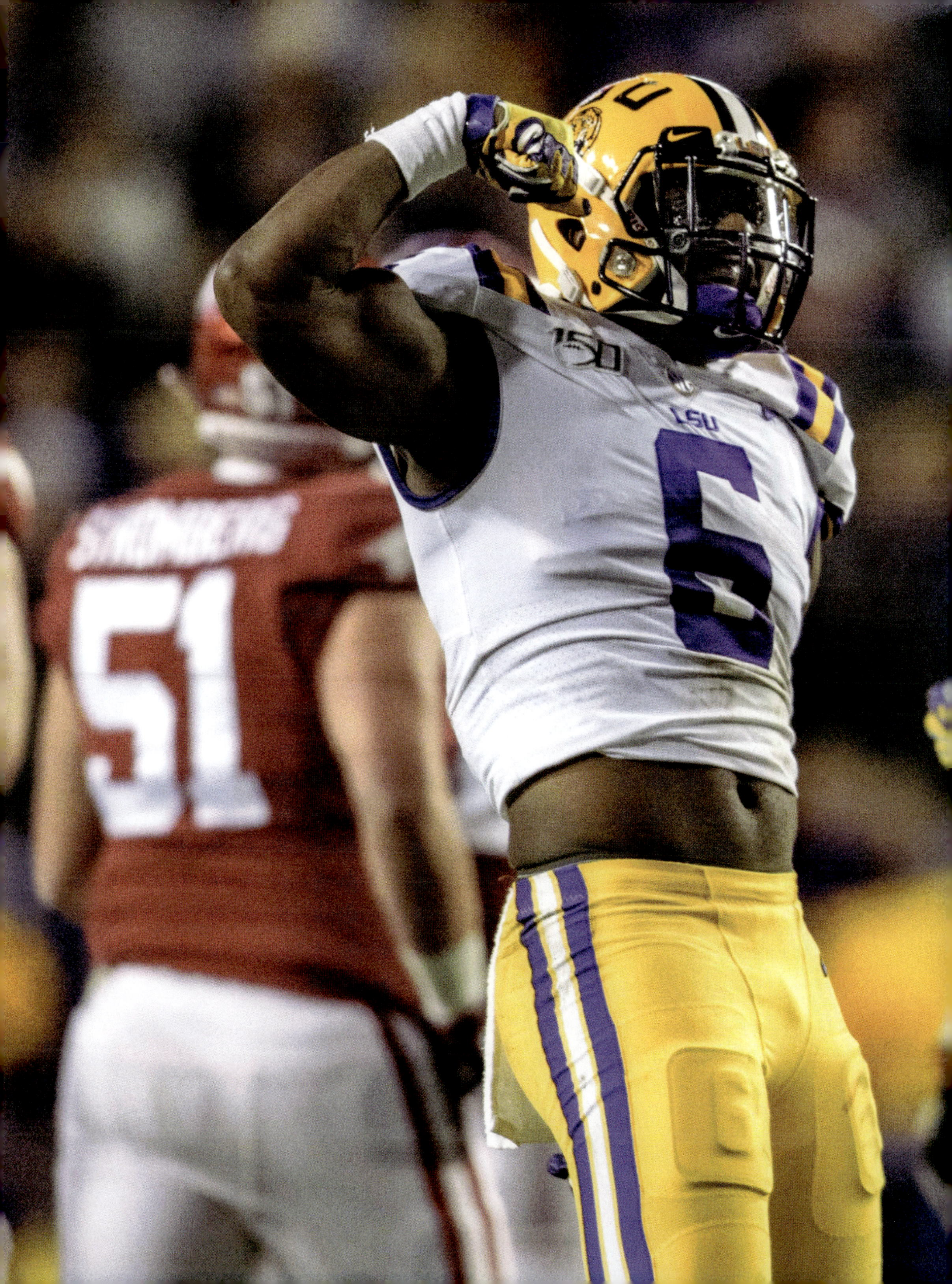
LSU
6
51

Tigers wide receiver Terrace Marshall Jr. (6) can't reel in a pass as Arkansas defensive back Greg Brooks Jr. (9) defends. MATTHEW HINTON / AP PHOTO

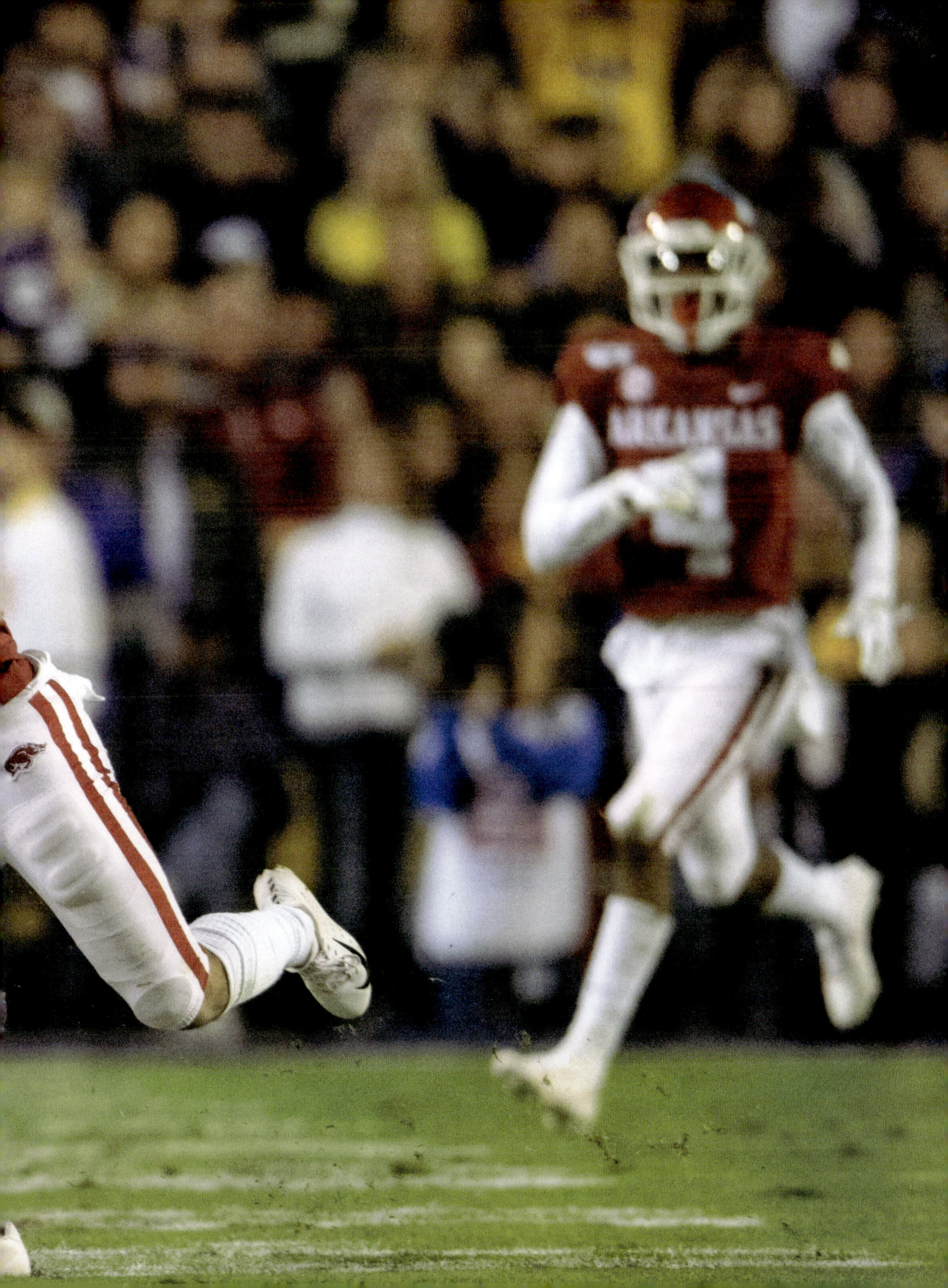

**ABOVE:** LSU running back Clyde Edwards-Helaire (22) breaks away from Arkansas defensive back Myles Mason (18) on his way to the end zone.  CHRIS GRAYTHEN / GETTY IMAGES

**OPPOSITE:** Head Coach Ed Orgeron celebrates as Tigers running back John emery Jr. scores on a 39-yard fourth quarter touchdown run.
MATTHEW HINTON / AP PHOTO

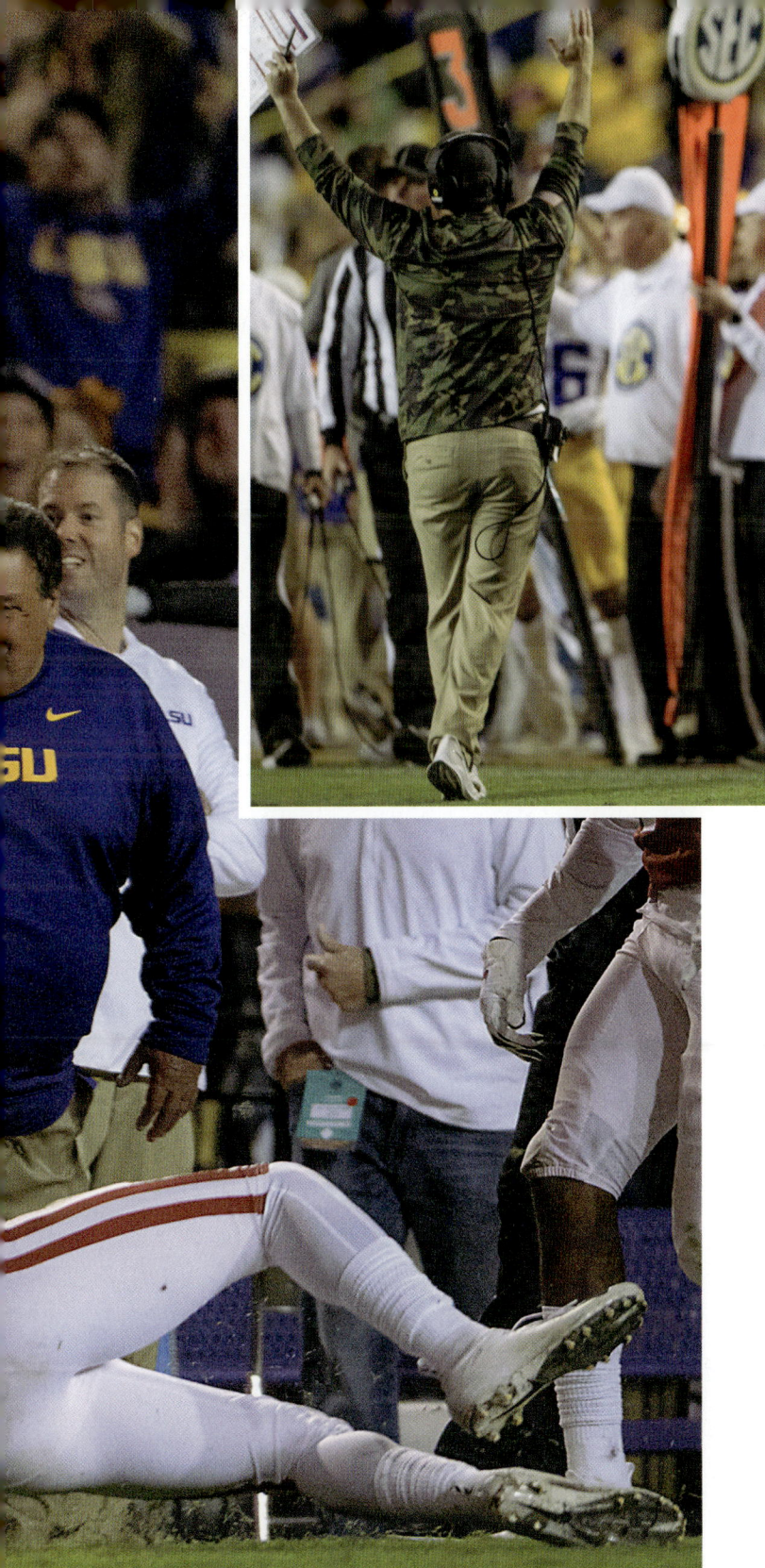

to Ja'Marr Chase on the game's first possession. They connected on a 50-yarder in the third quarter on which Burrow eclipsed 4,000 yards for the season and Chase increased in single-season LSU record for TD catches to 15.

Burrow's other touchdown toss was a 10-yarder on a crossing route to Justin Jefferson.

Interim Arkansas coach Barry Lunney Jr. started freshman quarterback KJ Jefferson, who exhibited potential and athleticism, if not consistency. Jefferson, the fourth starting QB for the Razorbacks this season, completed 7 of 14 passes for 105 yards without a turnover. He also looked effective rushing at times, but his total in that department was skewed by three sacks.

"He competed hard but we didn't have enough gas in our tank to hang with these guys for four quarters," Lunney said.

The Razorbacks (2-9, 0-7), who've lost eight straight, were as close as 7-6 in the second quarter after Jefferson led them to their second field goal — a 47-yarder by Connor Limpert.

That's when LSU began to pull away. Burrow completed four quick passes for 66 yards to set up Tyrion Davis-Price's 2-yard touchdown to make it 14-6. By halftime, the Tigers led 28-6. ■

# LSU 50, TEXAS A&M 7
### NOVEMBER 30, 2019 | BATON ROUGE, LOUISIANA

# Perfect Finale
## Burrow, No. 1 LSU dominate Texas A&M

Joe Burrows intention to give LSU fans one last memorable night in Tiger Stadium was as obvious as the name on the back of his jersey.

When the crowd realized during pregame introductions that it read, "Burreaux," a spelling evocative of Louisiana's Cajun French heritage, roars of approval poured forth from the Death Valley stands.

And that was just the beginning.

Burrow padded his Heisman Trophy resume with 352 yards and three touchdowns passing, and No.1 LSU beat Texas A&M 50-7 on Saturday night to give the Tigers their first unbeaten regular season since 2011.

"I thought it would just be an awesome tribute to the state, to the university," said Burrow, who'd largely grown up in Ohio and spent three seasons as a backup for Ohio State before transferring to LSU, where his football career took off. "It's been awesome not only for me, but for my family as well ... I'm going to miss it with all my heart and I couldn't be more grateful."

The crowd made certain Burrow knew the feeling was mutual, cheering wildly when coach Ed Orgeron ceremoniously called his star QB to the sideline for good after his 23rd completion early in the fourth quarter. Burrow raised his arms to salute the crowd before embracing coaches and teammates.

"Louisiana's a special place, man," Orgeron said. "LSU is special place. When you play for the Tigers, you're a Tiger."

"Joe's meant a lot to Louisiana," Orgeron added. "Louisiana is very proud of LSU football. People in Louisiana have heart, man. When they love you, they love you. And they love Joe, and Joe loves them. The guy's been phenomenal"

Burrow's highlights included a deep, pin-point accurate pass on a 78-yard touchdown to JaMarr Chase, who had 197 yards and two touchdowns on seven catches.

Burrow (who wore his regular jersey during the game) also hit Justin Jefferson with a 12-yard scoring pass, while his second scoring pass to Chase covered 18 yards.

Burrow has 4,366 yards and 44 touchdowns passing this season, smashing LSU single-season records in both categories. Burrow's yards passing total also broke the SEC record, which had stood since 1998. Burrow's 44 TDs has tied the SEC's single season mark set by Missouri's Drew Lock in 2017.

Last season, LSU and Texas A&M played seven overtimes before the Aggies prevailed, 74-72. LSU entered the week talking redemption and emphatically backed it up,

Tigers quarterback Joe Burrow (9) launches one of his three touchdown passes on the day. SEAN GARDNER / GETTY IMAGES

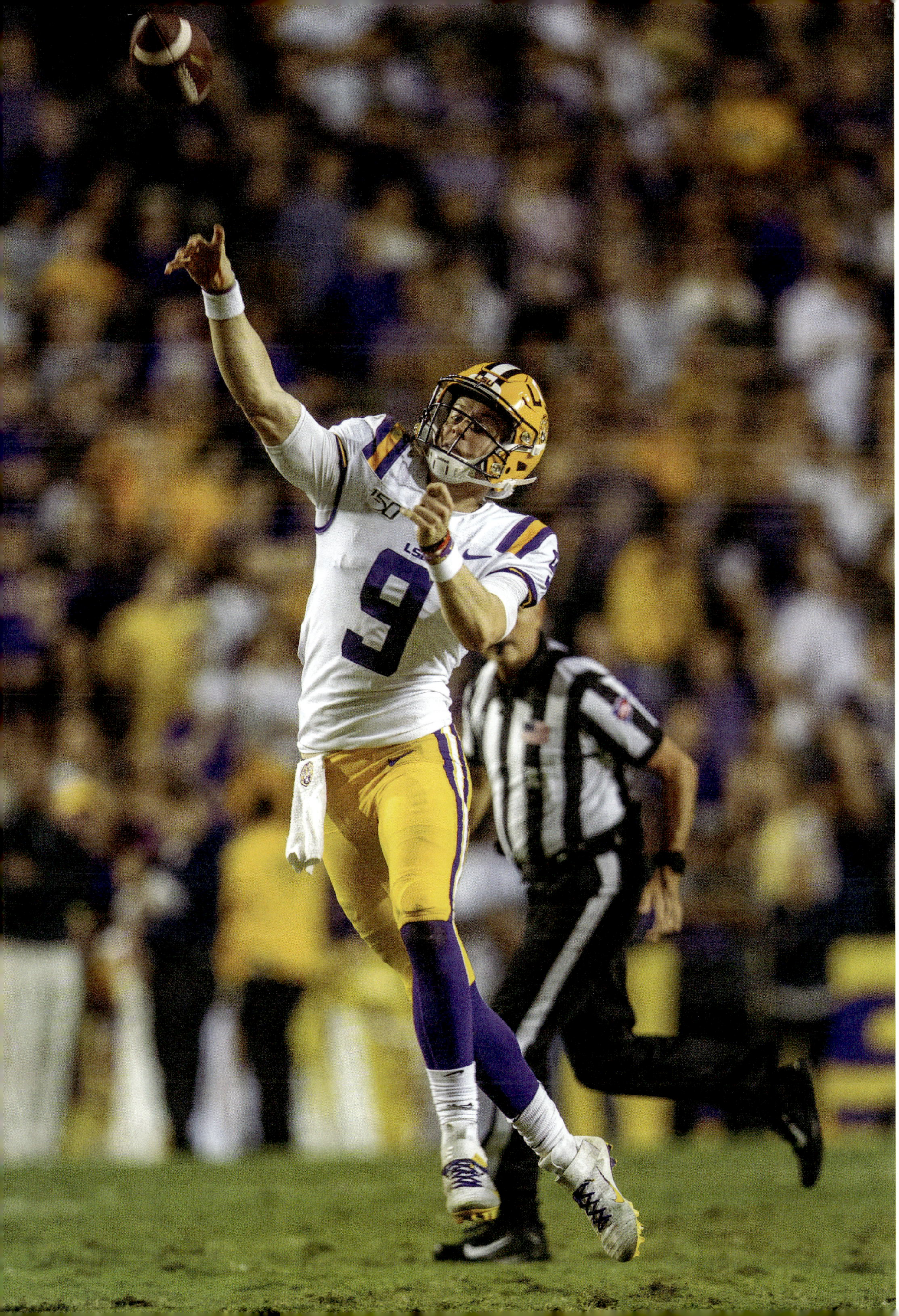

outgaining Texas A&M (7-5, 4-4) 553-169.

"The efficiency of our offense – I thought it'd be efficient, but not just as explosive and break all these records," Orgeron said. "We never thought about records."

"They kicked our butts," Aggies coach Jimbo Fisher said. "LSU's offense is outstanding."

Edwards-Helaire's 5-yard TD on LSU's opening possession began a first-half onslaught in which LSU scored on its first five possessions, racing to a 31-0 lead by halftime.

Kellen Mond completed just 10 of 30 passes for 92 yards and was intercepted three times— once each by Grant Delpit, Jacoby Stevens and Kary Vincent. Isaiah Spiller's 1-yard TD run provided the Aggies' only score.

"Kellen was pressured all night," Fisher said. "We couldn't get the running game going, couldn't get any first downs."

Stevens said LSU defensive players took note when the Tigers were dropped behind Ohio State in the CFP rankings last week, with inconsistent play by the LSU defense cited as a reason why.

"We took that as a challenge that we need to have a complete game and play for 60 minutes, and I feel like we did that today," Stevens said. "When a team averages as much yards as they do (419.6 yards per game coming in) and you hold them to less ... it always feel good because you dominate the game, you take over the game and you make somebody do something they don't want to do." ∎

**ABOVE:** Tigers wide receiver Ja'Marr Chase (1) celebrates his touchdown reception with teammates Saahdiq Charles (77) and Justin Jefferson (2). GERALD HERBERT / AP PHOTO

**OPPOSITE:** Tigers safety Marcel Brooks (9) sacks Texas A&M quarterback Kellen Mond (11). JOHN KORDUNER-ICON SPORTSWIRE / AP PHOTO

Quarterback Joe Burrow (9) gestures thanks to the student section after playing his last game in Tiger Stadium.
GERALD HERBERT / AP PHOTO

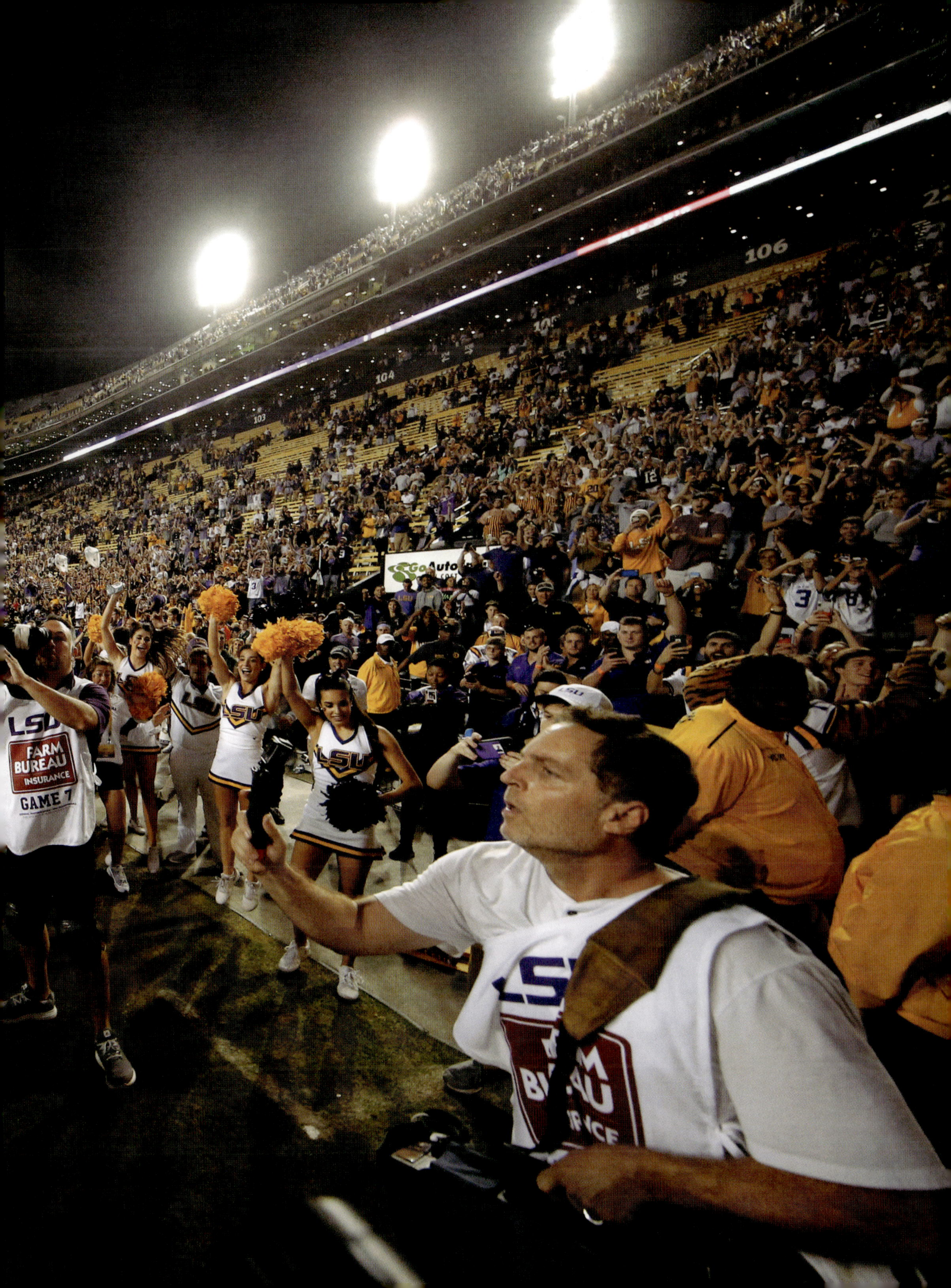

106
104
103
LSU
FARM
BUREAU
INSURANCE
GAME 7

# Heisman Winner

## Burrow first LSU player to win award in 60 years

Born into a family of Cornhuskers and raised in the Buckeye state, Joe Burrow left his roots behind and became a Heisman Trophy winner at Louisiana State.

The quarterback won the Heisman on Saturday night in a record-breaking landslide, becoming the first LSU player to bring college football's most prestigious award back to Baton Rouge in 60 years.

Burrow received 2,608 points and 841 first-place votes, a record 90.7% of all the first-place votes available. Burrow also set a record for percentage of points available received with 93.8, breaking the mark of 91.6% set by Troy Smith of Ohio State in 2006. Burrow was named on 95.5% of all ballots, breaking the record of 95.2% set by Oregon's Marcus Mariota in 2014.

Burrow's margin of victory of 1,846 broke the record of 1,750 set by O.J. Simpson of USC in 1968.

Oklahoma quarterback Jalen Hurts was second with 762 points. Quarterback Justin Fields of Ohio State was third, and defensive end Chase Young of Ohio State was fourth.

Burrow transferred last year to LSU from Ohio State, where he was a sparingly used reserve. After finishing strong for the Tigers in 2018, he broke out this season, setting a Southeastern Conference record with 48 touchdown passes and leading top-ranked LSU (13-0) to its first College Football Playoff appearance.

Burrow's victory was a foregone conclusion, but after he was announced as the winner it still overwhelmed him.

"That's the most I've cried in 23 years of living," Burrow said later.

After hugging his parents and coaches, Burrow made his way to the stage inside the PlayStation Theater in Times Square. He started his acceptance speech, stopped and took 23 seconds to compose himself.

"All my teammates have supported me, welcomed me with open arms. Kid from Ohio, come down to the Bayou and welcomed me as brothers," Burrow said, with about two dozen former Heisman winners standing behind him on stage.

"What a special moment," LSU coach Ed Orgeron said. "I thought Joe handled everything first class. It's the first time I've seen him get that emotional."

The Tigers will face No. 4 Oklahoma and Hurts on Dec. 28 at the Peach Bowl in Atlanta.

"I'm ready to get back to Baton Rouge and start practice on Monday," Burrow said.

Burrow, a senior, blended perfectly with first-year LSU passing game coordinator Joe Brady and produced the most prolific offense in school history. Playing in an offense similar to the one Drew Brees runs for the New Orleans Saints, Burrow has shown accuracy and quick decision-making similar to his childhood idol. With at least one game left, Burrow has passed for 4,715 yards and is completing 77.9% percent of his passes, on pace to set an NCAA record.

The kid who grew up thinking he might play basketball in college, has blossomed into the possible first overall pick in April's NFL draft, and LSU's second Heisman winner.

Halfback Billy Cannon won the Heisman for LSU in 1959. The 60-year gap between Heisman victories for LSU is the largest for any school with multiple winners.

Burrow is the 17th quarterback to win the Heisman since 2000, and the third straight QB to win the award after transferring, joining Oklahoma's Baker Mayfield (2017) and Kyler Murray (2018).

Burrow's dad, Jimmy Burrow, was a longtime college football coach, who played at Nebraska. He spent the last 14 years of his career as defensive coordinator at the Ohio University in Athens

TODD VAN ERNST / HEISMAN TRUST

*"What a special moment. I thought Joe handled everything first class. It's the first time I've seen him get that emotional."*
— LSU Head Coach Ed Orgeron

**ABOVE:** Burrow gets emotional during his acceptance speech. TODD VAN ERNST / HEISMAN TRUSST

**OPPOSITE:** Burrow poses with the Heisman Trophy and Head Coach Ed Orgeron. TODD VAN ERNST / HEISMAN TRUSST

before retiring to spend his weekends in Louisiana watching his son play.

Joe Burrow grew up in The Plains, Ohio. His older brothers both played at Nebraska.

His father's old boss, Ohio coach Frank Solich, hoped the youngest Burrow boy would play for the Bobcats, but Joe took off in high school. Burrow was Mr. Football in Ohio in 2014 and signed with Ohio State the next year.

In Columbus, Ohio, Burrow joined an already loaded quarterback room with J.T. Barrett, Cardale Jones and Braxton Miller. Burrow redshirted as a freshman and played a little in 2016.

In 2017, he was competing with Dwayne Haskins to be Barrett's backup and broke his hand in preseason practice. That opened the door for Haskins to position himself as the quarterback of the future for Ohio State.

After spring practice in 2018, having already graduated from Ohio State, Burrow decided to transfer. LSU wasn't his first choice, but Orgeron recruited the quarterback hard.

"He gave me an opportunity when not a lot of people thought i was going to do anything," Burrow said. "He trusted me with his program."

Burrow was interested in Nebraska, but that interest wasn't reciprocated. Cincinnati seemed like a possibility, playing for former Ohio State assistant coach Luke Fickell.

A visit to LSU, with its 100,000-seat stadium, rich history of winning, southern hospitality and SEC competition, won over Burrow. Orgeron has called Burrow his most important recruit and maybe the most important recruit in the history of LSU football.

That might have sounded like hyperbole a few months ago.

Not anymore.

"It's been a long and winding (journey)," Burrow said, "and there's still more chapters to be written." ∎

*Biletnikoff Award Winner    Ja'Marr Chase*

*Thorp Award Winner    Grant Delpit*

# LSU 37, GEORGIA 10
### DECEMBER 7, 2019 | ATLANTA, GEORGIA

# SEC CHAMPS!
## Burrow completes Heisman coronation, LSU routs Georgia

Joe Burrow collected a shiny award as the game's MVP.

LSU's fans had another trophy on their minds.

"Heisman! Heisman! Heisman!" they chanted.

The coronation is likely complete.

Burrow turned in another dazzling performance on the big stage, leading No. 1 LSU to a spot in the College Football Playoff with a 37-10 rout of No. 4 Georgia in the Southeastern Conference championship game.

"Joe is the heartbeat of this team," running back Clyde Edwards-Helaire said.

The Tigers, going for their first national title since 2007 season, will either return to Atlanta or head west to suburban Phoenix for a semifinal game on Dec. 28. They surely made a persuasive case to be the top overall seed when the four-team field and pairings are announced Sunday.

Burrow was all over the stat sheet for LSU (13-0, No. 2 CFP). He threw for 349 yards and four touchdowns. He was the Tigers' second-leading rusher with 41 yards on 11 carries, often leaving the Bulldogs grasping at air as he twirled this way and that. He even caught a pass on a ball that was batted down at the line and wound up his arms, taking off for a 16-yard gain.

"He's a great athlete, man," Georgia safety J.R. Reed said. "We had a lot of plays out there we were supposed to make, and he'd just squeeze out of it."

The Heisman-worthy moment came late in the third quarter. With Georgia (11-2, No 4 CFP) bringing the heat, Burrow spun to his left to get away from lineman Travon Walker, whirled back to his right to send Walker sprawling to the turf, then delivered a pass on the run while sprinting toward the LSU sideline with another defender in hot pursuit.

Justin Jefferson hauled in the throw just beyond midfield and took off down to the Bulldogs 9 for a 71-yard play. Three plays later, Burrow delivered his third TD pass of the game, hooking up with Terrace Marshall Jr., on a 4-yard touchdown pass that essentially finished off the Bulldogs.

"It was all improvised," Burrow said. "Justin ran a 6-yard hitch route and saw me scrambling and took off deep. We got a great feel for each other. I knew exactly where he was going to be when I got out of there."

Burrow wasn't done. Derek Stingley's second pick of Jake Fromm turned the ball back over to the prolific LSU offense at the 13, and Burrow wasted no time finding Jefferson for an 8-yard TD in the waning seconds of the third quarter to send many in the

Tigers quarterback Joe Burrow (9) runs away from Georgia defenders during second half action. KEVIN C. COX / GETTY IMAGES

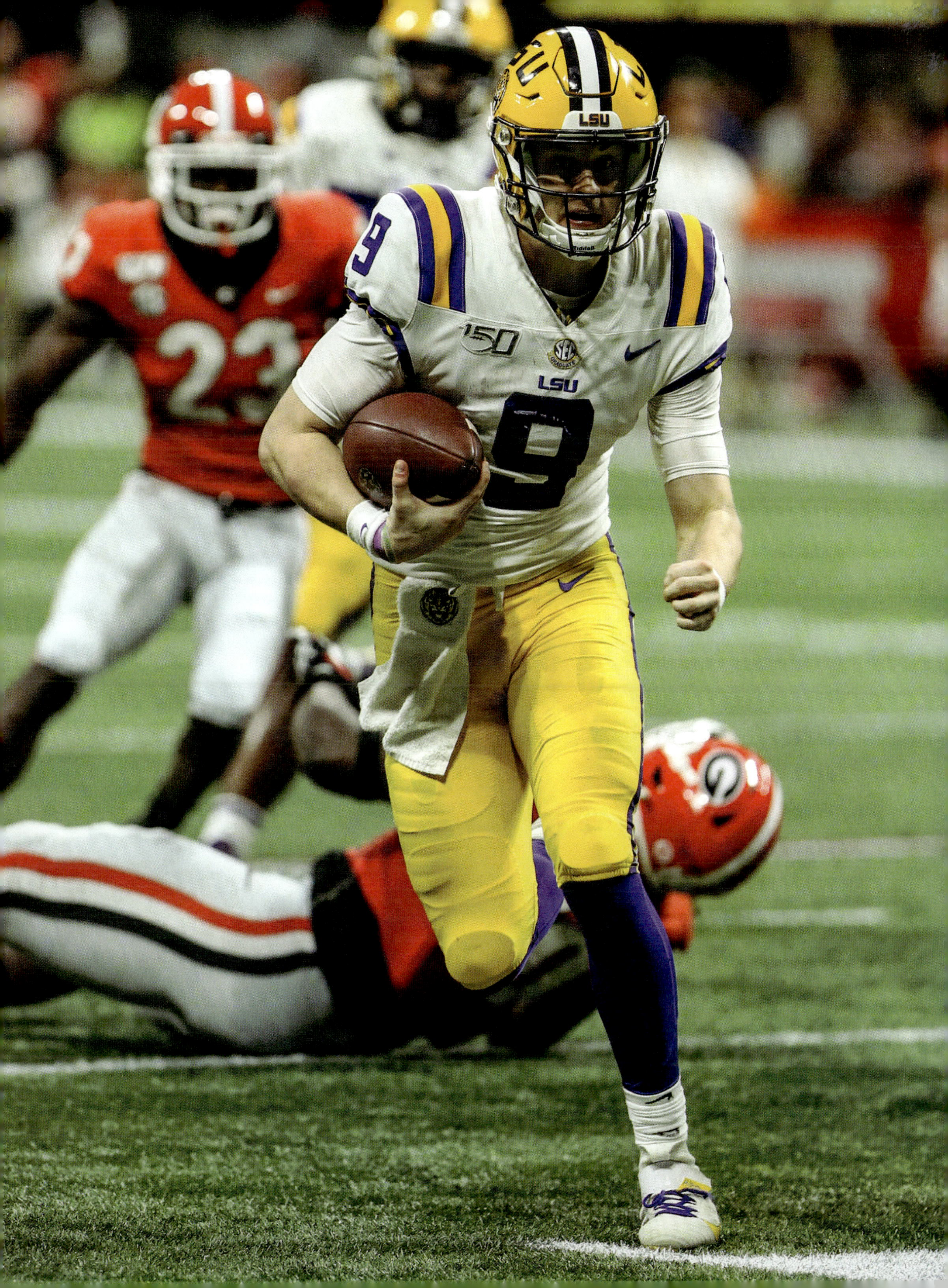
LSU
9
23

Tigers wide receiver Justin Jefferson (2) sprints away from two Georgia defenders as he scores on a 8-yard third quarter touchdown reception. JOHN BAZEMORE / AP PHOTO

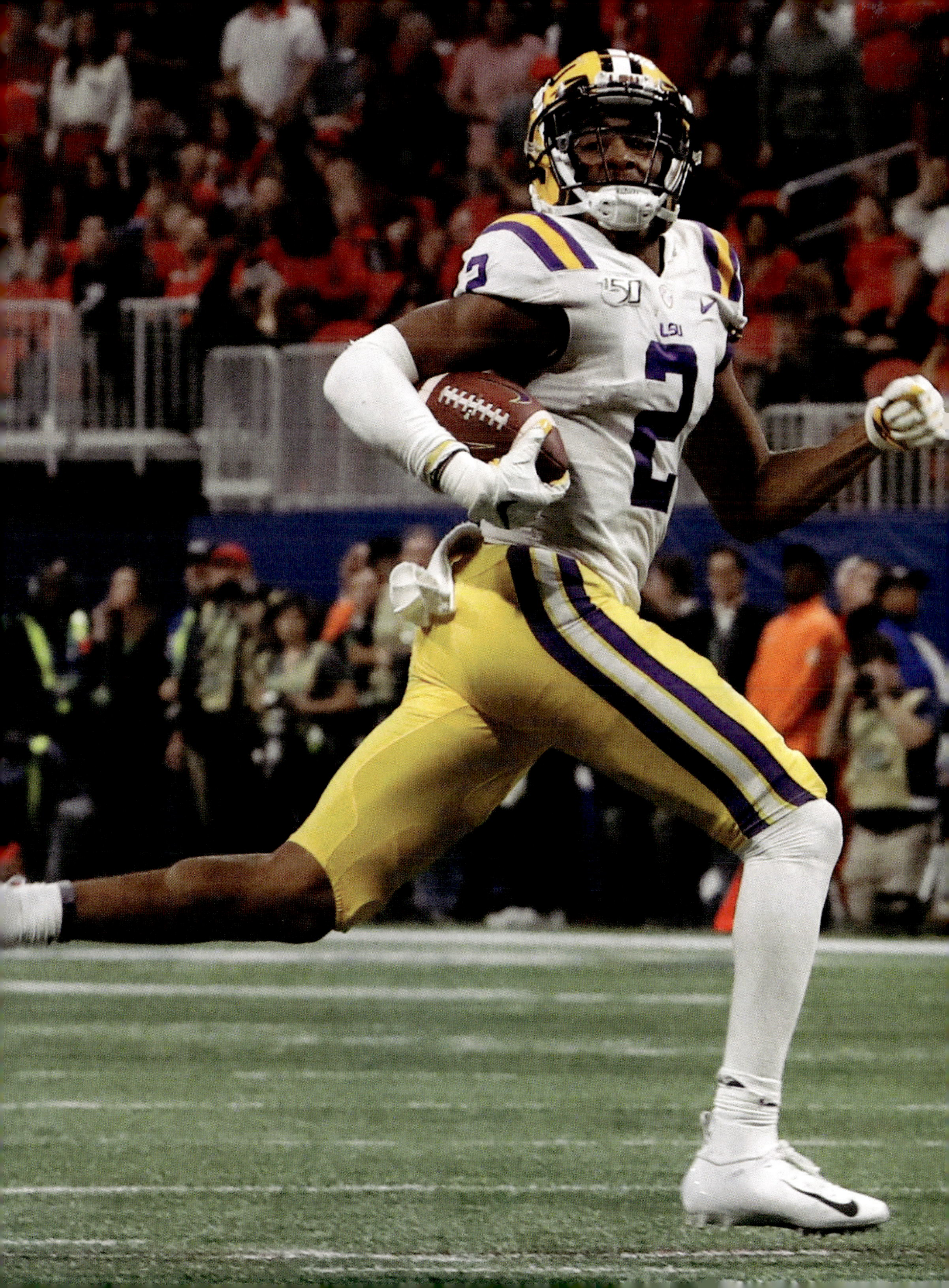
LSU

**ABOVE:** Tigers cornerback Derek Stingley Jr. (24) intercepts a pass intended for Georgia receiver George Pickens (1) in the third quarter.
TODD KIRKLAND / GETTY IMAGES

**RIGHT:** Joe Burrow and head coach Ed Orgeron celebrate.
JOHN BAZEMORE / AP PHOTO

**OPPOSITE:** Tigers safety Grant Delpit (7) sacks Georgia quarterback Jake Fromm (11). Fromm was injured on the play.
JOHN BAZEMORE / AP PHOTO

predominantly Georgia crowd heading for the exits.

LSU left no doubt it is the king of the mighty SEC, completing its run through a gauntlet of the league's top teams. The Tigers had already knocked off Alabama, Florida and Auburn. Now, they can add the Bulldogs to the list, ensuring the SEC will only get one team in the national playoff.

LSU came into the game as the second-highest scoring team in the country behind Ohio State. They figured to have a tougher time against Georgia's stellar defense, ranked No. 2 in points allowed. but Burrow kept the Bulldogs on their heels the entire game.

It was by far the most points Georgia has given up this season. Until Saturday, they held every opponent under 20 except South Carolina, which stunned the Bulldogs in double overtime nearly two months ago.

There was no such drama in this one.
Just total domination by the Tigers.
It was a painful loss — literally — for the Bulldogs, who were making their third straight appearance in the SEC title game. Two players were carted off the field with apparently major injuries. Another player wobbled off with a concussion after being leveled on a kickoff. Fromm twisted an ankle and had to go to the medical tent to get taped up, though he missed only one play.

Not that it mattered.

Fromm, who guided Georgia to the cusp of the national title two years ago as a freshman, was 20 of 42 for 225 yards with those two interceptions. He didn't get much help from his teammates: Tyler Simmons dropped a deep ball on the very first possession, and Matt Landers couldn't hang on to a throw in the end zone.

Georgia finally reached the end zone with just under 12 minutes remaining on Fromm's 2-yard TD pass to George Pickens.

"That is a really good football team," coach Kirby Smart said. "We were going to have to make explosive plays. We were unable to do that." ∎

LSU players celebrate after winning the SEC Championship game. TODD KIRKLAND / GETTY IMAGES

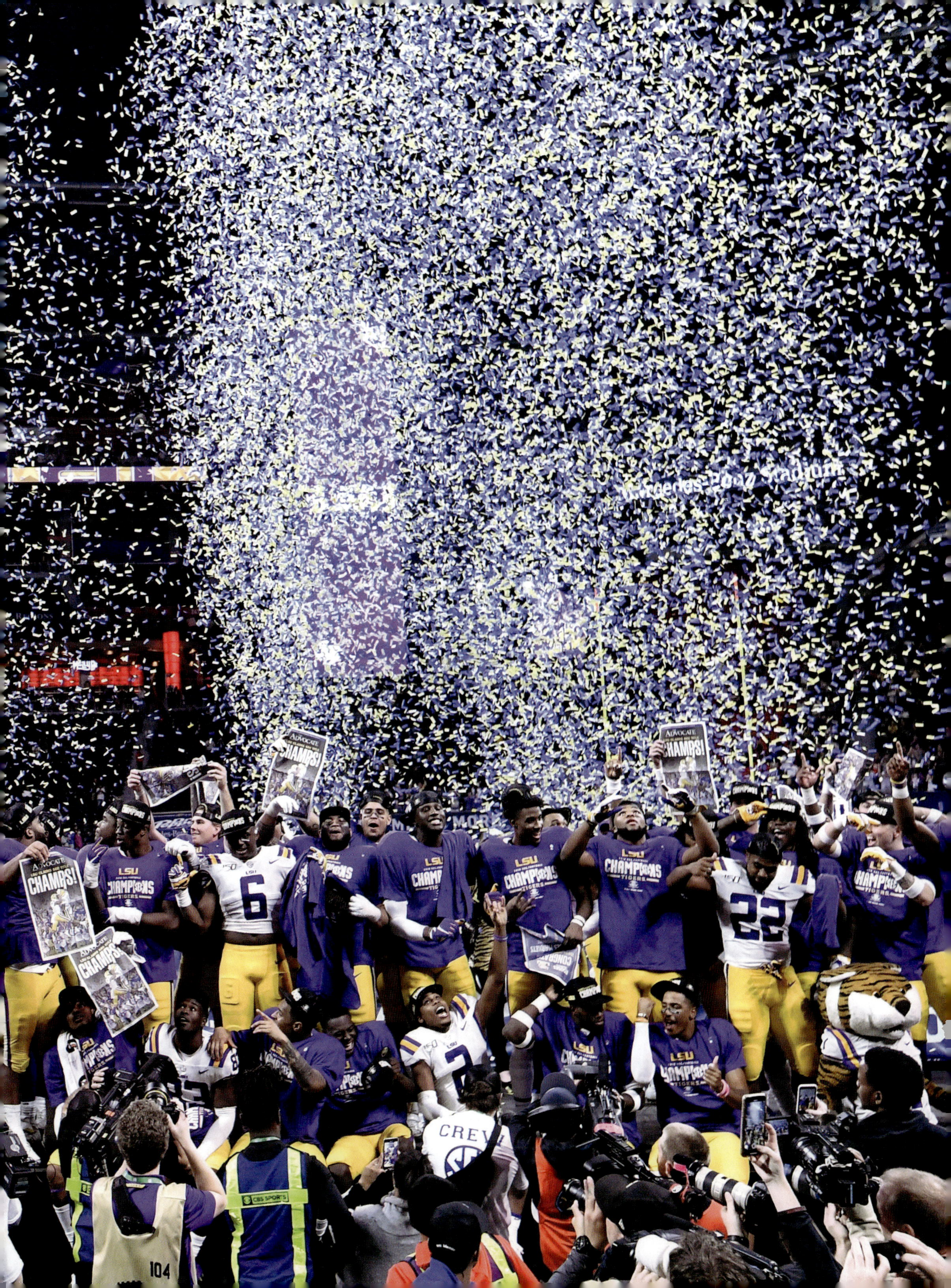
ADVOCATE
CHAMPS!
LSU
CHAMPIONS
TIGERS
CBS SPORTS
104

## LSU 63, OKLAHOMA 28
DECEMBER 28, 2019 | ATLANTA, GEORGIA

# No. 1 LSU routs Oklahoma

The Tigers are on to the national championship game after a record-setting night by Joe Burrow and Co.

Joe Burrow and the LSU Tigers turned in a first half for the ages, a breathtaking offensive display even as their coordinator grieved a horrific tragedy from his box high above the field.

This team from the bayou is truly something special.

With one more victory, it will be a national champion.

In his first game as a Heisman Trophy winner, Burrow threw for seven touchdowns and 493 yards as No. 1 LSU romped to a stunning 63-28 victory over No. 4 Oklahoma in the Peach Bowl semifinal game Saturday.

The Tigers (14-0) are headed to the title game against No. 3 Clemson -- a 29-23 winner over No. 2 Ohio State in the second semifinal in Arizona -- clicking on all cylinders, having dismantled the Sooners (12-2) with a 30-minute outburst that will long be remembered in Cajun country.

"We go into every game thinking nobody can stop us," Burrow said.

Certainly, the Sooners couldn't.

Burrow tied the record for any college bowl game with his seven TD passes -- which all came before the bands hit the field for the halftime show at Mercedes-Benz Stadium. Justin Jefferson was on the receiving end for four of those scoring plays, also tying a bowl record.

As if that wasn't enough, Burrow scored an eighth TD himself on a 3-yard run in the third quarter, thoroughly dominating his expected duel with Oklahoma quarterback Jalen Hurts, the Heisman runner-up.

Yet, the postgame celebration was weighed down by heavy hearts.

LSU offensive coordinator Steve Ensminger learned shortly before kickoff that his daughter-in-law, broadcaster Carley McCord, was among five people killed in a plane crash in Louisiana. The small plane went down shortly after takeoff for what was supposed to be a flight to Atlanta for the game.

Head coach Ed Orgeron delivered the news to Ensminger, who was seen with tears running down his cheeks but stuck to the task at hand.

"Coach, we're going to get through this," Emsminger told his boss.

Then the coordinator headed to his usual spot in the box, calling plays alongside passing game coordinator Joe Brady.

It was a brilliant, poignant performance in the face of such grief. The players didn't learn until afterward what Ensminger was going through.

Justin Jefferson (2) celebrates the touchdown by the Tigers tight end Thaddeus Moss (81). GREGORY SHAMUS / GETTY IMAGES

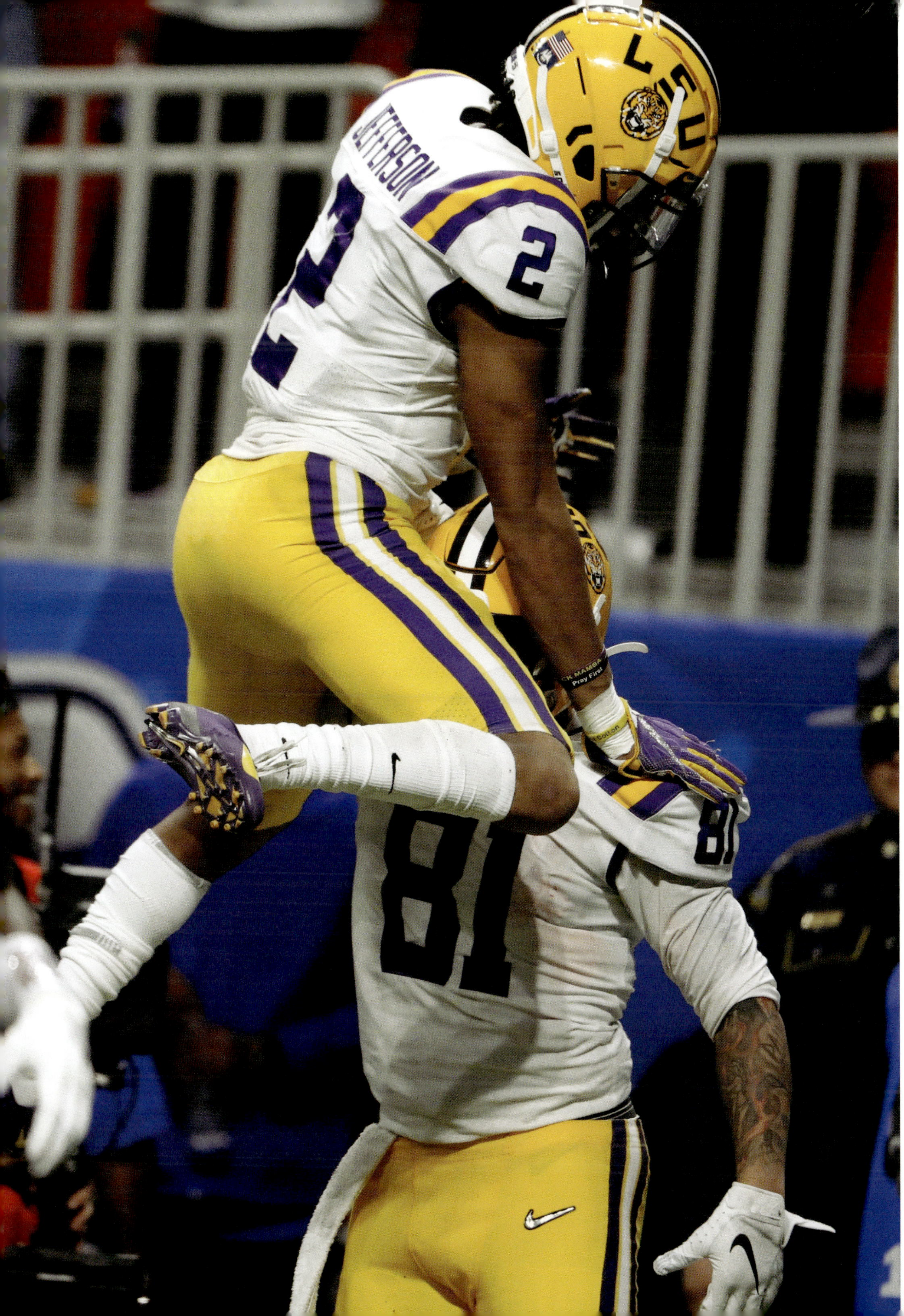
2
81

Tigers quarterback Joe Burrow (9) rolls out and looks downfield during first half action. Burrow threw for 493 yards and 7 touchdowns on the day. JOHN BAZEMORE / AP PHOTOS

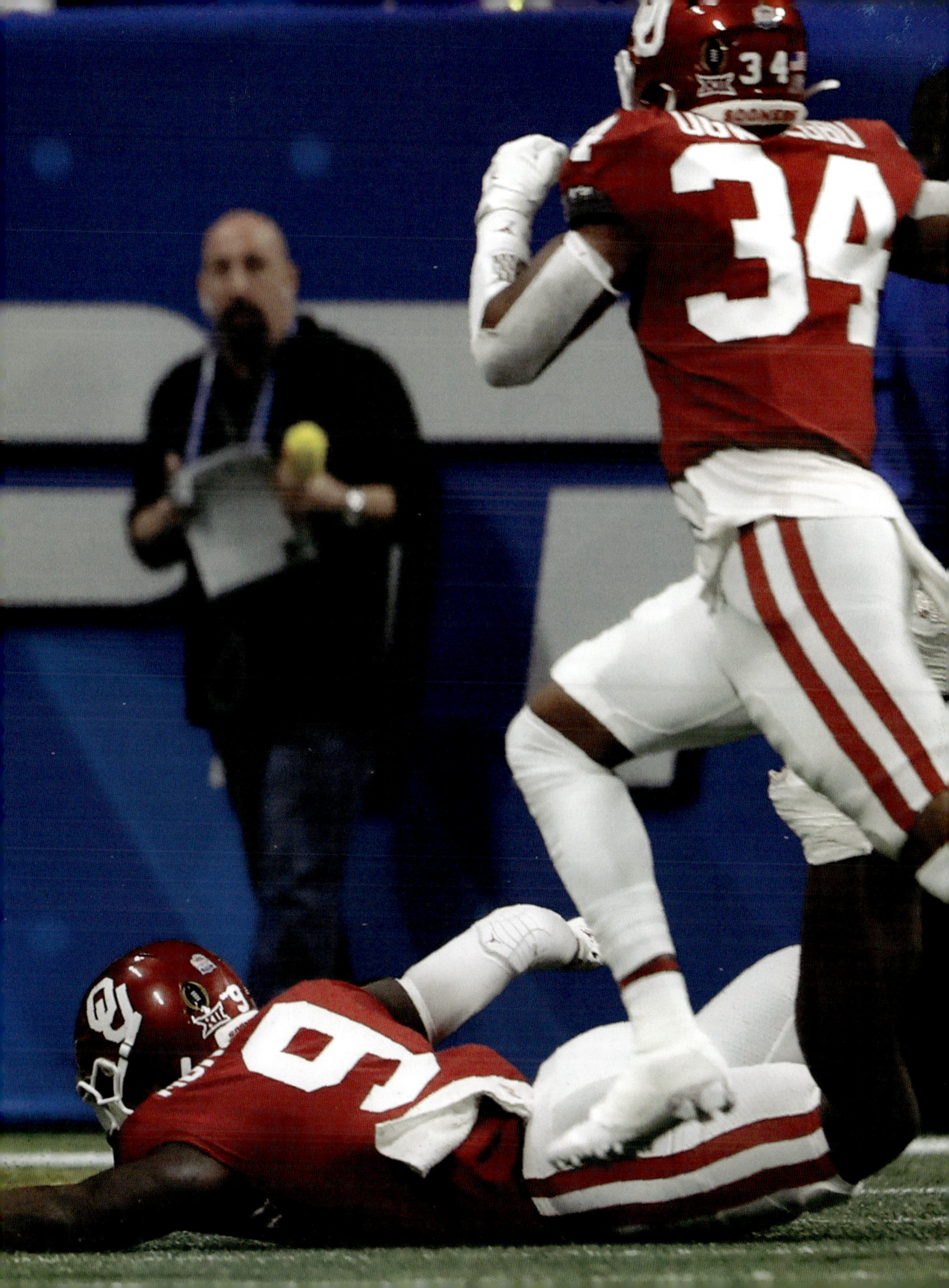

"I can't think of what he was able to do today with the circumstances," Brady said. "It speaks to the type of man he is."

LSU needed only three plays to race 42 yards for its first score — a perfectly thrown ball over Jefferson's shoulder for a 19-yard TD less than 3 minutes into the game.

Oklahoma briefly put up a fight. Hurts' 51-yard pass to CeeDee Lamb set up a 3-yard touchdown run by Kennedy Brooks that tied the score at 7.

After that, the rout was on.

It was 49-14 by halftime.

The Tigers' potent spread offense made this one look much like the Harlem Globetrotters carving up the Washington Generals, only it was the Sooners playing the hapless victim.

Jefferson hauled in a 35-yard pass for touchdown No. 2. Then a 42-yarder for No. 3. And, finally, a 30-yard scoring strike that left him counting off four fingers for the crowd — all before the midway point of the second quarter.

Terrace Marshall Jr. contributed to the onslaught with TD catches of 8 and 2 yards. Tight end Thaddeus Moss — the son of NFL Hall of Fame receiver Randy Moss — made his daddy proud by getting free behind the secondary, hauling in a pass and shoving off a fast-closing defender to complete the 62-yard scoring play.

"One team, one heartbeat," Orgeron said.

It was a miserable finale for Hurts, who closed out a nomadic college career that began with him leading Alabama to a pair of national championship games before losing his starting job to Tua Tagovailoa. After graduating, Hurts transferred to Oklahoma for a one-and-done season that produced some dazzling numbers but ended short of the ultimate goal.

Running for his life most of the game, Hurts was largely stymied on

Wide receiver Justin Jefferson (2) hauls in a 35-yard first quarter touchdown catch to put the Tigers up 21-7. GREGORY SHAMUS / GETTY IMAGES

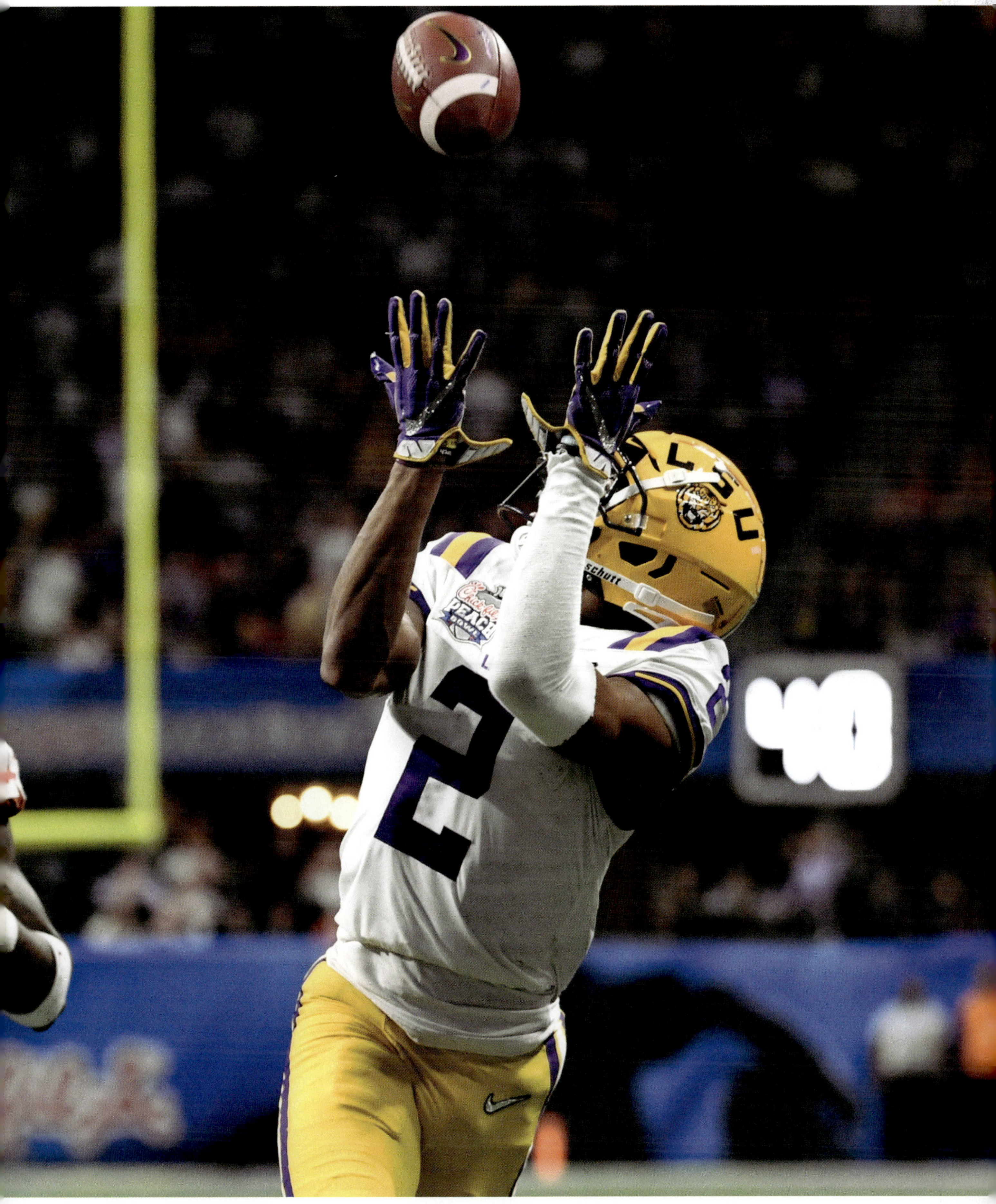
LSU
schutt
PEACH
BOWL
2

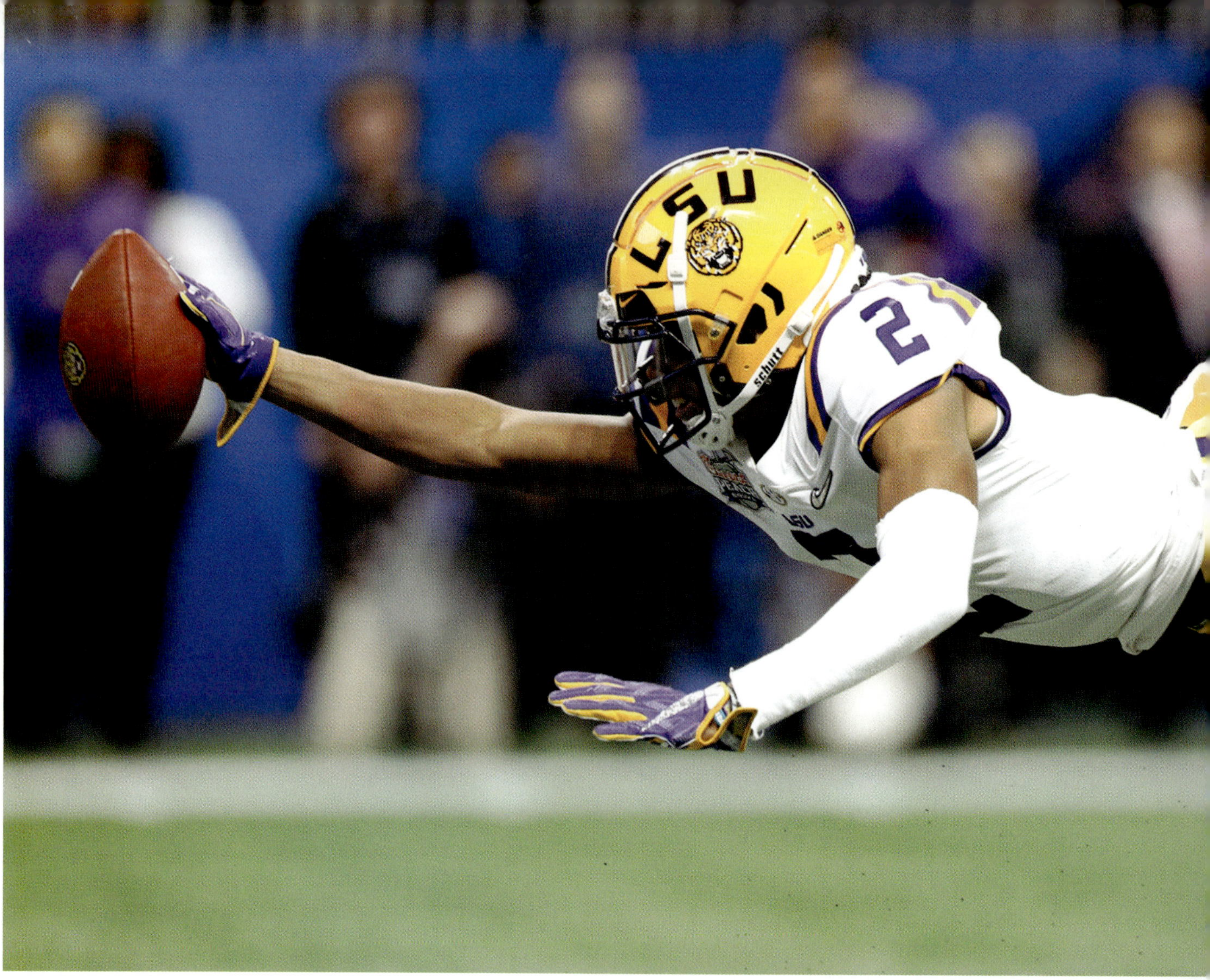
LSU

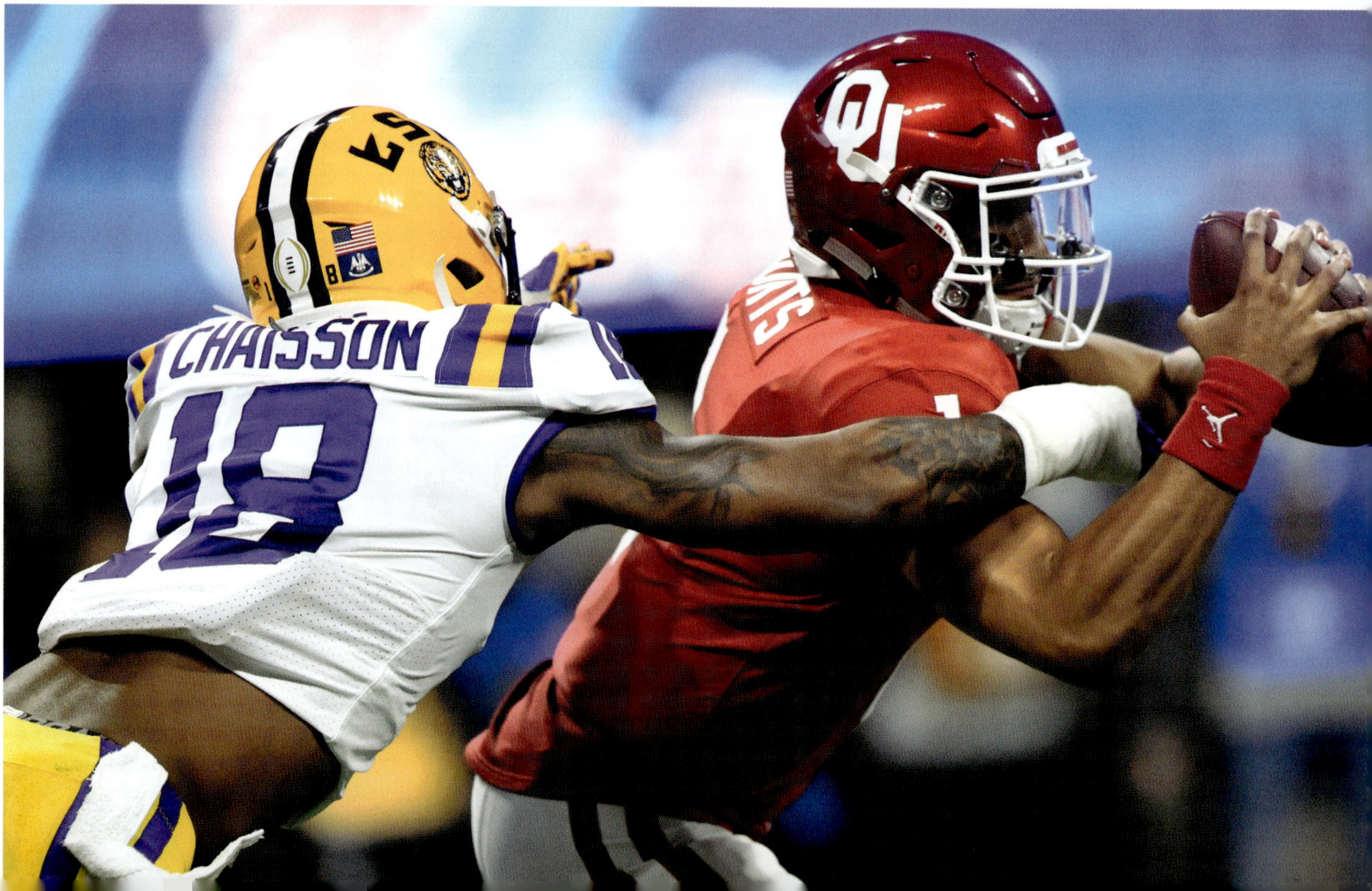
CHAISSON
18

the ground and through the air. He ran for a pair of touchdowns but gained just 43 yards with his legs. He was held to 15 of 31 for 217 yards passing, giving up a brilliant, leaping interception to Kary Vincent Jr. that quickly brought the LSU offense back on the field as the Tigers were blowing the game open.

"We needed to take advantage of every opportunity we had against a team like this," Hurts said. "We failed to do that."

"They did not really run their base stuff," LSU defensive coordinator Dave Aranda said. "I think they were trying to trick us and gadget us. When those things didn't hit, that gave us some downs that we executed on. It gave us some juice."

Does it tell you something when a team won't run their base stuff?

"Yes, yes," Aranda said. "By the time they kind of settled in … there was already a rhythm and flow to the game. The scoreboard was tilted in our favor by that point." ∎

**LEFT:** Tigers wide receiver Justin Jefferson (2) extends for a touchdown while Oklahoma safety Pat Fields (10) attempts to tackle him. KEVIN C. COX / GETTY IMAGES

**LOWER LEFT:** Tigers linebacker K'Lavon Chaisson (18) sacks Oklahoma quarterback Jalen Hurts (1) during the first half. JOHN AMIS / AP PHOTO

**BELOW:** Joe Burrow advances LSU on the championship board. CARMEN MANDATO / GETTY IMAGES

LSU Tigers celebrate a Chick-fil-A Peach Bowl CFP Semifinal game victory. TODD KIRKLAND / GETTY IMAGES

PLAYOFF
SEMIFINAL
CHAMPS
LSU
18
Chick-fil-A
PEACH
BOWL
PLAYOFF

# 2019 ROSTER

| NO. | NAME | POS. | HT. | WT. | CLASS | EXP. | HOMETOWN |
|---|---|---|---|---|---|---|---|
| 1 | Ja'Marr Chase | WR | 6-1 | 200 | So. | 1L | Harvey, La. |
| 1 | Kristian Fulton | CB | 6-0 | 200 | Sr. | 2L | New Orleans, La. |
| 2 | Justin Jefferson | WR | 6-3 | 192 | Jr. | 2L | St. Rose, La. |
| 3 | AJ Aycock | QB | 6-5 | 212 | Fr. | RS | Jonesboro, Ark. |
| 3 | Tyrion Davis-Price | RB | 6-1 | 226 | Fr. | HS | Baton Rouge, La. |
| 3 | JaCoby Stevens | S | 6-1 | 228 | Jr. | 2L | Murfreesboro, Tenn. |
| 4 | John Emery Jr. | RB | 6-0 | 203 | Fr. | HS | St. Rose, La. |
| 4 | Todd Harris Jr. | S | 5-11 | 190 | Jr. | 2L | Maringouin, La. |
| 5 | Devonta Lee | WR | 6-1 | 223 | Fr. | HS | Fluker, La. |
| 5 | Kary Vincent Jr. | S | 5-10 | 185 | Jr. | 2L | Houston, Texas |
| 6 | Terrace Marshall Jr. | WR | 6-4 | 200 | So. | 1L | Bossier City, La. |
| 6 | Jacob Phillips | LB | 6-4 | 233 | Jr. | 2L | Nashville, Tenn. |
| 7 | Grant Delpit | S | 6-3 | 203 | Jr. | 2L | Houston, Texas |
| 8 | Peter Parrish | QB | 6-1 | 190 | Fr. | HS | Phenix City, Ala. |
| 8 | Patrick Queen | LB | 6-1 | 227 | Jr. | 2L | Ventress, La. |
| 9 | Marcel Brooks | S | 6-2 | 194 | Fr. | HS | Ft. Worth, Texas |
| 9 | Joe Burrow | QB | 6-4 | 216 | Sr. | 1L | Athens, Ohio |
| 10 | Stephen Sullivan | TE | 6-5 | 242 | Sr. | 3L | Donaldsonville, La. |
| 11 | Eric Monroe | S | 6-1 | 208 | Jr. | 1L | Houston, Texas |
| 12 | Walker Kinney | QB | 6-2 | 218 | Fr. | HS | Stilwell, Kan. |
| 12 | Donte Starks | LB | 6-1 | 217 | Fr. | HS | Marrero, La. |
| 13 | Jontre Kirklin | WR | 6-0 | 185 | Jr. | 2L | Lutcher, La. |
| 14 | Mo Hampton Jr. | S | 6-0 | 214 | Fr. | HS | Memphis, Tenn. |
| 14 | John Gordon McKernan | QB | 6-2 | 186 | Fr. | HS | Baton Rouge, La. |
| 15 | Myles Brennan | QB | 6-4 | 207 | So. | 1L | Long Beach, Miss. |
| 16 | Jay Ward | CB | 6-2 | 167 | Fr. | HS | Moultrie, Ga. |
| 17 | Racey McMath | WR | 6-3 | 221 | Jr. | 1L | New Orleans, La. |
| 18 | K'Lavon Chaisson | OLB | 6-4 | 250 | So. | 1L | Houston, Texas |
| 19 | Derrick Dillon | WR | 5-11 | 186 | Sr. | 3L | Franklinton, La. |
| 22 | Clyde Edwards-Helaire | RB | 5-8 | 209 | Jr. | 2L | Baton Rouge, La. |
| 22 | Zaven Fountain | S | 6-3 | 171 | Fr. | RS | Marrero, La. |
| 23 | Micah Baskerville | LB | 6-1 | 228 | So. | 1L | Shreveport, La. |
| 23 | Corren Norman | RB | 5-9 | 191 | Fr. | HS | Broussard, La. |
| 24 | Chris Curry | RB | 6-0 | 215 | Fr. | RS | Lehigh Acres, Fla. |
| 24 | Derek Stingley Jr. | CB | 6-1 | 190 | Fr. | HS | Baton Rouge, La. |
| 25 | Cordale Flott | CB | 6-2 | 160 | Fr. | HS | Saraland, Ala. |
| 25 | Josh Williams | RB | 5-10 | 192 | Fr. | HS | Houston, Texas |
| 26 | Keenen Dunn | RB | 6-0 | 180 | So. | TR | Gonzales, La. |
| 29 | Raydarious Jones | CB | 6-2 | 161 | Fr. | HS | Horn Lake, Miss. |
| 30 | Cade Comeaux | DB | 6-0 | 178 | Fr. | RS | New Orleans, La. |
| 30 | Jack Mashburn | TE | 6-3 | 207 | Fr. | HS | Covington, La. |
| 31 | Cameron Lewis | S | 6-2 | 197 | Jr. | SQ | Monroe, La. |
| 31 | Thomas McGoey | WR | 6-0 | 187 | Fr. | HS | Thibodaux, La. |
| 32 | Avery Atkins | PK | 5-11 | 217 | So. | 1L | Auburn, Ala. |
| 33 | Trey Palmer | WR | 6-1 | 180 | Fr. | HS | Kentwood, La. |
| 34 | Lloyd Cole | CB | 6-0 | 200 | Jr. | RS | Bossier City, La. |
| 34 | Connor Culp | PK | 5-10 | 187 | Jr. | 1L | Phoenix, Ariz. |
| 35 | Damone Clark | LB | 6-3 | 239 | So. | 1L | Baton Rouge, La. |
| 36 | Cade York | PK | 6-2 | 189 | Fr. | HS | McKinney, Texas |
| 38 | Zach Von Rosenberg | P | 6-5 | 240 | Jr. | 2L | Zachary, La. |
| 39 | Mason Bruns | PK | 5-10 | 167 | Fr. | HS | Fort Walton Beach, Fla. |
| 41 | Carlton Smith | LB | 6-3 | 243 | So. | SQ | Houston, Texas |
| 42 | Hunter Faust | LB | 6-1 | 232 | Fr. | RS | New Orleans, La. |
| 42 | Aaron Moffitt | TE | 6-2 | 252 | So. | SQ | Baton Rouge, La. |
| 43 | Preston Stafford | PK | 5-11 | 164 | Fr. | HS | Baton Rouge, La. |
| 43 | Ray Thornton | OLB | 6-3 | 227 | Jr. | 2L | Killeen, Texas |
| 44 | Tory Carter | FB | 6-1 | 250 | Jr. | 2L | Valdosta, Ga. |
| 44 | Dylan Thompson | OLB | 6-1 | 258 | Fr. | HS | Irving, Texas |
| 45 | Michael Divinity Jr. | OLB | 6-2 | 241 | Sr. | 3L | Marrero, La. |
| 45 | Stephen King | TE | 6-6 | 228 | Fr. | RS | Alexandria, Va. |
| 46 | Andre Anthony | OLB | 6-4 | 250 | Jr. | 1L | New Orleans, LA. |
| 47 | Nelson Jenkins III | DL | 6-4 | 286 | Fr. | RS | Maringouin, La. |
| 47 | Quentin Skinner | SNP | 6-0 | 253 | Fr. | HS | Buford, Ga. |
| 48 | Blake Ferguson | SNP | 6-3 | 235 | Sr. | 3L | Smyrna, Ga. |
| 49 | Jansen Mayea | TE | 6-3 | 239 | Fr. | RS | New Iberia, La. |
| 49 | Travez Moore | DE | 6-4 | 246 | Jr. | RS | Bastrop, La. |
| 51 | Dare Rosenthal | OT | 6-7 | 314 | Fr. | RS | Clayton, La. |
| 52 | Tayte Langley | LB | 6-3 | 245 | Fr. | HS | Iota, La. |
| 53 | Soni Fonua | OLB | 6-3 | 274 | Jr. | JC | Salt Lake City, Utah |
| 54 | Aaron Benfield | LB | 6-2 | 230 | Fr. | HS | Thibodaux, La. |
| 55 | Jarell Cherry | DE | 6-3 | 264 | Fr. | RS | Dallas, Texas |
| 57 | Chasen Hines | OG | 6-3 | 336 | So. | 1L | Marshall, Texas |
| 58 | Jared Small | LB | 6-0 | 213 | So. | SQ | Baton Rouge, La. |
| 58 | Kardell Thomas | OL | 6-3 | 329 | Fr. | HS | Baton Rouge, La. |
| 59 | Desmond Little | OLB | 6-5 | 210 | Fr. | HS | Prichard, Ala. |
| 61 | Cameron Wire | OT | 6-6 | 300 | Fr. | RS | Gonzales, La. |
| 62 | Siaki Ika | NT | 6-4 | 354 | Fr. | HS | Salt Lake City, Utah |
| 63 | Michael Smith | OL | 6-2 | 325 | Jr. | SQ | Killeen, Texas |
| 64 | Austin Harden | OL | 6-1 | 310 | Fr. | HS | Patterson, La. |
| 65 | Jakori Savage | OL | 6-6 | 294 | Jr. | 2L | Bay Minette, Ala. |
| 68 | Damien Lewis | OG | 6-3 | 332 | Sr. | 1L | Canton, Miss. |
| 69 | Charles Turner | OL | 6-4 | 266 | Fr. | HS | Canton, Ohio |
| 70 | Ed Ingram | OG | 6-4 | 295 | So. | 1L | Desoto, Texas |
| 71 | Donavaughn Campbell | OL | 6-5 | 360 | Jr. | 1L | Ponchatoula, La. |
| 72 | Tyler Shelvin | NT | 6-3 | 346 | So. | 1L | Lafayette, La. |
| 73 | Adrian Magee | OL | 6-4 | 343 | Sr. | 3L | Franklinton, La. |
| 74 | Badara Traore | OT | 6-7 | 320 | Sr. | 1L | Boston, Mass. |
| 75 | Anthony Bradford | OL | 6-7 | 355 | Fr. | HS | Muskegon, Mich. |
| 76 | Austin Deculus | OL | 6-7 | 322 | Jr. | 2L | Mamou, La. |
| 77 | Saahdiq Charles | OT | 6-4 | 295 | Jr. | 2L | Jackson, Miss. |
| 78 | Thomas Perry | OL | 6-6 | 341 | Fr. | HS | Lafayette, La. |
| 79 | Lloyd Cushenberry III | C | 6-4 | 315 | Jr. | 2L | Carville, La. |
| 80 | Jamal Pettigrew | TE | 6-6 | 258 | Jr. | 1L | New Orleans, La. |
| 81 | Thaddeus Moss | TE | 6-3 | 249 | Jr. | SQ | Charlotte, N.C. |
| 82 | Brandon Hubicz | TE | 6-2 | 197 | Fr. | HS | Baton Rouge, La. |
| 83 | Jaray Jenkins | WR | 6-4 | 195 | Fr. | RS | Jena, La. |
| 84 | TK McLendon | DE | 6-5 | 263 | Jr. | JC | Soperton, Ga. |
| 85 | Ray Parker | OLB | 6-5 | 233 | Fr. | HS | Ruston, La. |
| 86 | Michael Martin | WR | 5-9 | 174 | Fr. | RS | Weslaco, Texas |
| 87 | Evan Francioni | WR | 6-0 | 194 | Fr. | RS | River Ridge, La. |
| 88 | Alex Aucoin | WR | 6-0 | 180 | Fr. | RS | Baton Rouge, La. |
| 89 | Colby Brunet | WR | 6-0 | 194 | Jr. | 1L | Metairie, La. |
| 90 | Rashard Lawrence | DL | 6-2 | 308 | Sr. | 3L | Monroe, La. |
| 91 | Breiden Fehoko | DL | 6-2 | 291 | Sr. | 1L | Honolulu, Hawaii |
| 92 | Neil Farrell Jr. | DE | 6-4 | 298 | Jr. | 2L | Mobile, Ala. |
| 93 | Justin Thomas | DE | 6-5 | 256 | Jr. | 1L | Daphne, Ala. |
| 94 | Joseph Evans | DL | 6-2 | 288 | Fr. | HS | Haynesville, La. |
| 97 | Glen Logan | DE | 6-4 | 309 | Jr. | 2L | Kenner, La. |